1000 Tin Toys

1000 Tin Toys

Teruhisa Kitahara
Yukio Shimizu

TASCHEN

KÖLN LISBOA LONDON NEW YORK OSAKA PARIS

Front cover / Umschlagvorderseite / Couverture:
1950s, *Mr. Atomic*, Yonezawa, 155 x 175 x 225 mm
Spine / Buchrücken / Dos:
1950s, *Astronaut*, Yonezawa, 95 x 125 x 240 mm
Back cover / Umschlagrückseite / Dernière de Couverture:
1950s, *1958 Lincoln Mark III Continental, 1959 Cadillac,*
Bandai, 295 x 105 x 75, 280 x 105 x 175 mm

Die Bildlegenden enthalten folgende Angaben:
Entstehungszeit, Titel, Hersteller, Maße
(Tiefe, Breite, Höhe)

The captions contain the following information:
Date of production, title, manufacturer, size
(depth, width, height)

Les légendes donnent les indications suivantes:
Date de fabrication, titre, marque, dimensions
(profondeur, largeur, hauteur)

© 1996 Benedikt Taschen Verlag GmbH
Hohenzollernring 53, D–50672 Köln
© 1996 for the illustrations: Teruhisa Kitahara;
Photos by Yukio Shimizu
Design by Burkhard Riemschneider, Cologne
Edited by Christiane Blaß/Ute Kieseyer, Cologne
English translation: Deborah ffoulkes, Cologne
French translation: Michèle Schreyer, Cologne
German translation: Hanae Kamachi, Plattensen

Printed in Italy
ISBN 3–8228–8856–7

Contents

Inhalt

Sommaire

Introduction
Teruhisa Kitahara

Who hasn't had one of these in their hands, at least as a child – the tin aeroplanes and ships, the clockwork robots or the big American limousines?

It was not only these and other tin toys which the toy cupboards contained, however. They were also home to a colourful medley of many childhood dreams and longings. Today, these tin toys can transport us back to our childhood, they call up a vision of a time we thought we had already forgotten.

"Buriki", the Japanese word for tin, is derived from "blik", which is the Dutch word for it. Around 1874, the Japanese imported the first tin plate for the manufacture of oil canisters, boxes and cans. And when the first tin toys arrived in the country – for example, locomotives and steamships from Germany – it provided Japanese companies with the impetus to start producing these toys themselves. Soon, rickshaws, goldfish and tortoises made of tin appeared in the Japanese shops. The toy manufacturing industry got off to a slow start, but after the end of the war between Japan and China in 1894, the boom started.

Highly sophisticated tin printing and punching machines were introduced and Japan soon became one of the world's largest producers of tin toys. There were also a number of set-backs, however: in 1928, production had to be stopped due to the unstable political and economic situation, and World War II put a stop to the progress of the tin toys, at least for a while. Nevertheless, production started up again as early as 1945, with Japan under American occupation, and railways, fire engines and the first clockwork tin toys were available again for export.

The production of tin toys reached its peak in the fifties – in such numbers and of such a quality, the likes of which have never been seen again. During the same period, the first electrically-driven toys conquered the market. In 1963, tin toys constituted 60 per cent of Japanese toy exports, but towards the end of the sixties, plastic ousted tin from its leading position. Today, now that computer games have made their entrance into the playroom, tin toys have become practically obsolete.

I spent my youth in the fifties, the golden age of tin toys, and they were part and parcel of my childhood. Unfortunately, however, I later forgot about them completely. Then, at the age of twenty-five, I saw them again: I visited a friend, a designer, who had a few tin toys lying around the house, which he used as decorations – and this is what started me off. I was simply enthralled and fascinated by the powerful colours and shapes, and a warm feeling of nostalgia went though me from head to foot. From that day onwards, I have been crazy about tin toys.

I got hold of my first piece in an old toy shop, redolent of tradition. It was a bright red fire engine which was collecting dust in a corner. I bought it for 180 yen, which was about half a dollar. From then on, I was in toy shops almost every day, and bought everything I could lay my hands on. I was practically insatiable, and the larger my collection became, the more toys I wanted to possess. The result: after one and a half years, my house was full to bursting point with tin toys. It may sound strange, but I am in love with them. When I came home in the evening, tired after a hard day's work, and saw my tin toys waiting there, it reinvigorated me, and today they still have the same effect on me.

Before I was bitten by the collecting bug, I went skiing in the Austrian town of Innsbruck. There I stayed with a family, and in their house, hung on the walls, were old pans which had been used for cooking for generations. I was struck by how much these people valued hand-crafted products. In contrast to Europe, where old objects, like pieces of furniture, for example, are taken great care of and handed down from generation to generation, Japan is governed by a throw-away mentality, and people there have no respect for implements used in daily life. I myself, however, feel personally responsible for every one of my tin toys, and uphold the tradition of preserving such objects.

Although tin toys are mass-produced articles, they possess many of the characteristics of hand-crafted ones. They comprise approximately 200, sometimes up to 300 individual parts, which were assembled by hand. The body, doors and manufacturer's mark of a tin car, for example, had to be individually stamped, and a separate pressing mould was required for every detail, be it ever so small. Today's plastic toys do not evince even a fraction of the intricacy of the tin ones in their heyday. To manufacture them in the same manner would be far too costly, and in any case, there are currently no workers available with the requisite skills. When I hold a tin toy in my hand, I can feel the expertise, love and careful which these craftsmen put into their little tin works of art. Today, the tin toys also bear witness to history; they have survived wars and crises, and tell us something of the fashions, colours and preferences of their time. Even after 22 years, this continues to fascinate me.

When the number of toys in my collection reached 10,000, I allowed a department store to use them for a television advertising spot: in the deep of the night, when all is still and everyone is asleep, the toys suddenly start to move and they have a huge party. Just before the sun rises, they go back to their usual places and stiffen again, just as if nothing had happened. At the International Film Festival in Cannes, this spot was awarded a bronze prize.

The film made my collection famous, and from then on I presented them in many exhibitions. One of these exhibitions drew more than 36,000 visitors in only two weeks. The large numbers of visitors surprised me, and gave me the idea of founding a museum to enable me to share the magic of the tin toys with many more people. That was twelve years ago.

In April 1986, the dream came true – the first "Toys Club" museum in Yokohama opened its doors to the public. More museums were founded in the years which followed, and the next on my list – the seventh – is the "Antique Toy World Museum". There, I plan to exhibit "Character Dolls", tin figures in the vein of Walt Disney's creations, Popeye, and Charlie Chaplin – an enormous toy wonderland. I have organised exhibitions outside Japan also, in Los Angeles and San Francisco, and books of photographs have been published on the history of tin toys.

It has recently become more difficult to find beautiful old pieces, which means that I am all the more thrilled and happy when I discover a rare toy. I believe that many people indulge in a passion for collecting because in this way they can continually expand and enlarge the world which they themselves have discovered. I myself have not only further added to my collection but have also, through the years, got to know many people and have had the most interesting encounters.

The toys often suffer a sad fate: some are simply thrown away by those ignorant of their worth, some are forgotten and left behind in the playground, and still others are tossed on the rubbish heap by dealers because they don't sell. If I find toys like this, I take them home and clean them thoroughly of all the rust and dirt. Then I polish them with oil, and the shiny surface seems to give the toys a new lease of life. In this manner, a neglected piece of tin is transformed into an antique.

In the meantime, I have been collecting for 22 years, and will continue to do so in the future, rescuing tin toys and keeping them safe in my museums, where they can show the world how beautiful they are. I am firmly convinced that this is my task in life, and nothing makes me more happy than when people view my collection and discover the magic of the tin toys.

Einführung
Teruhisa Kitahara

Wer hat sie nicht schon einmal in der Hand gehabt, und sei es als Kind –
die Flugzeuge und Schiffe aus Blech, die Roboter zum Aufziehen oder
die großen amerikanischen Straßenkreuzer? Die Spielzeugkisten früherer Tage bewahrten, neben diesen und
anderen Gegenständen auch eine bunte Welt verschiedenster Kinder-
träume und -sehnsüchte. Heute können uns diese »Tin Toys« in unsere
Kindheit zurückversetzen, sie rufen uns eine Zeit vor Augen, die wir
längst vergessen glaubten.
»Buriki«, das japanische Wort für Blech, ist vom Niederländischen
»blik« abgeleitet. Um das Jahr 1874 importierten die Japaner die ersten
Blechplatten zur Herstellung von Ölkanistern, Büchsen und Konserven-
dosen. Und als das erste Blechspielzeug ins Land kam, beispielsweise
Lokomotiven und Dampfschiffe aus Deutschland, war das der Start-
schuß für die japanische Spielzeugproduktion. Bald sah man in den japanischen Geschäften Rikschas, Goldkarpfen und Schildkröten aus
Blech. Die zunächst nur zögernd anlaufende Spielzeugfertigung erlebte
1894, nach dem Ende des japanisch-chinesischen Krieges, eine Blütezeit.
Hochentwickelte Blechdruck- und -stanzmaschinen wurden einge-
führt – im Jahre 1906 zum Beispiel die sogenannte »Deutsche Feder« –,
und schon bald zählte Japan weltweit zu den größten Produzenten von
Blechspielzeug. Aber es gab auch Rückschläge: 1928 mußte die Produktion wegen der unsicheren politischen und wirtschaftlichen Situation
eingestellt werden, und der Zweite Weltkrieg stoppte zumindest für
eine gewisse Zeit den Vormarsch der Tin Toys. Doch schon 1945, noch
unter amerikanischer Besatzung, kam die Produktion von Blechspielzeug wieder in Gang: Eisenbahnen, Feuerwehrautos und die ersten Tin
Toys zum Aufziehen wurden exportiert.
In den 50er Jahren erreichte die Produktion von Blechspielzeug,
sowohl hinsichtlich der Qualität als auch hinsichtlich der Stückzahlen
einen absoluten Höhepunkt, und die ersten elektrisch betriebenen Spielzeuge eroberten den Markt. Im Jahre 1963 machten die Tin Toys etwa
60 Prozent des japanischen Spielzeugexports aus, bevor gegen Ende der
60er Jahre der Kunststoff das Blech von der Spitzenposition verdrängte.
Heute, da die Computerspiele Einzug in die Kinderzimmer gehalten

haben, sind Blechspielzeuge beinahe ganz in Vergessenheit geraten. Ich bin in den 50er Jahren, dem Goldenen Zeitalter der Tin Toys, aufgewachsen. Blechspielzeug war ein wesentlicher Bestandteil meiner Kindertage, den ich jedoch als Heranwachsender zunächst aus den Augen verlor. Erst im Alter von 25 Jahren begegnete ich den Tin Toys unvermittelt wieder: Ich besuchte einen Freund, einen Designer, der zu Dekorationszwecken Blechspielzeug in seiner Wohnung aufgestellt hatte. Dies war der zündende Funke. Ich war einfach hingerissen und fasziniert von den kräftigen Farben und Formen; ein Gefühl von Nostalgie durchrieselte meinen ganzen Körper, und seit diesem Tag bin ich einfach verrückt nach Blechspielzeug. Mein erstes Stück ergatterte ich in einem altehrwürdigen Spielzeugladen. Es war ein knallroter Feuerwehrwagen, der in einer Ecke verstaubte. Ich kaufte ihn für 180 Yen, umgerechnet gerade mal ein halber Dollar. Seitdem konnte man mich nahezu täglich in Spielzeugläden finden, wo ich alles kaufte, was mir in die Hände fiel. Ich war geradezu unersättlich, und je größer meine Sammlung wurde, desto mehr Spielzeug wollte ich in meinen Besitz bringen. Das Ergebnis: Nach anderthalb Jahren warmein Haus bis unters Dach mit Tin Toys vollgestopft. Es mag merkwürdig klingen, aber ich hatte mich in dieses Spielzeug aus Blech verliebt. Wenn ich abends erschöpft nach Hause kam und meine Tin Toys vor mir sah, lebte ich auf, und so geht es mir auch heute noch.

Einige Zeit bevor ich zum leidenschaftlichen Sammler wurde, hielt ich mich zum Skiurlaub in Innsbruck auf. Untergebracht war ich bei einer Familie, in deren Haus noch die alten Töpfe an den Wänden hingen, die über Generationen zum Kochen benutzt worden waren. Ich war tief beeindruckt, welche Wertschätzung in Europa handwerklichen Erzeugnissen entgegengebracht wird. Alte Gegenstände, beispielsweise Möbel, werden mit größter Sorgfalt gepflegt und weitervererbt, während in Japan eine absolute Wegwerfmentalität herrscht. Jede Ehrfurcht vor Gebrauchsgegenständen ist dort unbekannt. Ich hingegen fühle mich für jedes einzelne meiner Blechspielzeuge verantwortlich und stehe in dieser Tradition des Bewahrens.

Obwohl Blechspielzeuge Massenprodukte sind, haben sie mit Handwerkserzeugnissen einiges gemein. Sie bestehen aus rund 200, manchmal bis zu 300 Einzelteilen, die per Hand zusammengesetzt wurden. Für ein Blechauto mußten beispielsweise die Karosserie, die Türen und das Markenzeichen auf der Motorhaube einzeln gestanzt werden, und für jedes noch so winzige Detail war ein besonderer Stempel nötig. Das Plastikspielzeug von heute erfordert in der Herstellung nicht einen Bruchteil der Geschicklichkeit von einst, und eine solche Fertigung wäre derzeit auch unbezahlbar, ganz abgesehen davon, daß es keine entsprechend ausgebildeten Handwerker mehr gibt. Wenn ich ein Tin Toy in die Hand nehme, spüre ich dagegen das Können, die Liebe und Sorgfalt, mit der die Handwerker ihr kleines Kunstwerk aus Blech gefertigt haben.

Die Blechspielzeuge sind Zeugen der Geschichte, sie haben Kriege und Krisen überlebt und erzählen uns etwas von den Moden, Farben und Vorlieben ihrer Zeit – was mich auch heute noch nach über 20 Jahren Sammlertätigkeit fasziniert.

Als meine Spielzeugsammlung mehr als 10 000 Exemplare umfaßte, stellte ich sie einem Warenhaus für einen Fernseh-Werbespot zur Verfügung: Mitten in der Nacht erwachen die Spielzeuge plötzlich zum Leben und feiern eine riesige Party. Kurz vor Sonnenaufgang kehren sie an ihre angestammten Plätze zurück und erstarren wieder, als ob nichts geschehen wäre.

Durch diesen Film, der bei den Internationalen Filmfestspielen in Cannes die Auszeichnung in Bronze erhielt, wurde meine Sammlung in der Öffentlichkeit bekannt. Fortan präsentierte ich sie in vielen Ausstellungen; eine davon lockte in nur zwei Wochen mehr als 36 000 Interessierte an. Die überraschend hohe Besucherzahl brachte mich auf den Gedanken, ein Museum zu gründen, um vielen Menschen den Zauber der Blechspielzeuge zu vermitteln.

Im April 1986 war es dann soweit: Das erste »Toys Club«-Museum in Yokohama öffnete seine Pforten. Es folgten weitere Gründungen in den nächsten Jahren, und bald steht die Eröffnung des »Antique Toy World Museum«, des siebten Museums, bevor. In diesem riesiges Spielzeug-Wunderland werden »Character Dolls« zu sehen sein, Blechfiguren, die der Welt Walt Disneys, Popeyes und Charlie Chaplins entlehnt sind. Auch außerhalb Japans, in Los Angeles und San Francisco, habe ich Ausstellungen realisiert und darüber hinaus Fotobücher zur Geschichte des Blechspielzeugs veröffentlicht. In letzter Zeit ist es schwierig geworden, schöne alte Stücke zu finden. Um so größer ist mein Glücksgefühl, und mein Pulsschlag steigt, wenn ich ein seltenes Spielzeug entdecke.

Ich glaube, viele Menschen frönen der Sammelleidenschaft, weil sie auf diese Weise eine Welt, die sie selbst entdeckt haben, ständig erweitern und vergrößern können. Ich habe über die Jahre nicht nur meine Kollektion immer weiter vervollständigt, sondern auch interessante Begegnungen gehabt und viele Menschen kennengelernt.

Spielzeuge haben oft ein trauriges Schicksal: Manche werden in Unkenntnis ihres Wertes achtlos weggeworfen, andere werden auf dem Spielplatz vergessen, und wieder andere landen auf dem Müll weil sie unverkäuflich sind. Finde ich solche Spielzeuge, nehme ich sie mit nach Hause und reinige sie gründlich von Rost und Schmutz. Dann poliere ich sie mit Öl, und in ihrem neuen Glanz erwachen die Spielzeuge wieder zum Leben. So wird aus einem lange mißachteten Stück Blech eine Antiquität.

Auch nach 22 Sammlerjahren sehe ich mich immer noch berufen, Tin Toys vor der Zerstörung zu bewahren und in meinen Museen zu hüten, um den folgenden Generationen die Schönheit des Blechspielzeugs nahezubringen. Ich bin der festen Überzeugung, daß dies meine Lebensaufgabe ist, und es gibt keine schönere Vorstellung für mich, als daß immer mehr Menschen meine Sammlung ansehen und den Zauber der Tin Toys entdecken.

Préface
Teruhisa Kitahara

Vous les avez tenus au moins une fois dans votre main quand vous étiez enfant les avions et les bateaux en fer-blanc, les robots à remonter ou les belles américaines. En plus des jouets en fer-blanc et autres, les caisses à joujoux abritaient un pêle-mêle bigarré de rêves et de désirs enfantins. Les Tin Toys nous remettent en mémoire une époque que nous pensions avoir oubliée, et grâce à eux nous pouvons revivre notre enfance. «Buriki», c'est le terme japonais pour «fer-blanc», vient du néerlandais «Blik». Vers 1874, les Japonais ont importé les premières tôles en fer-blanc pour fabriquer des bidons d'huile, des récipients et des boîtes à conserves. Et lorsque les premiers jouets en fer-blanc firent leur apparition au Japon, des locomotives et des bateaux à vapeur fabriqués en Allemagne par exemple, ce fut le signal de départ pour la production japonaise de jouets. On vit bientôt des pousse-pousse, des poissons rouges et des tortues en fer-blanc dans les magasins nippons. La fabrication de jouets, fluctuante au début, connut son plein essor en 1894, après la guerre sino-japonaise.

On importa des machines à découper et imprimer la tôle très performantes – en 1906, par exemple, la «Deutsche Feder», un appareil allemand –, et le Japon devint bientôt l'un des plus importants fabricants mondiaux de jouets en fer-blanc. Mais il y eut aussi des moments difficiles: en 1928, la situation politico-économique était précaire et il fallut stopper la production, puis vint la Seconde Guerre mondiale qui interrompit de nombreuses années durant la fabrication des Tin Toys. Pourtant, celle-ci reprit déjà en 1945, alors que le pays était encore occupé par les Américains, et les trains, les voitures de pompiers et les premiers jouets en fer-blanc à remonter purent à nouveau être exportés.

La production des jouets en fer-blanc a connu son apogée dans les années 50 – ce haut standard de qualité et le nombre de pièces fabriquées ne furent plus jamais atteints –, et les premiers jouets électriques ont conquis le marché. En 1963, les jouets en fer-blanc constituaient 60 pour cent des exportations japonaises de jouets, mais vers la fin des années 60, les matières plastiques supplantèrent le fer-blanc. Aujourd'hui, les enfants sont fascinés par les jeux électroniques et les jouets en fer-blanc ont sombré dans l'oubli.

Je suis un enfant des années 50, l'Age d'or des «Tin Toys». Ils faisaient partie intégrante de ma vie. Plus tard, j'ai malheureusement oublié où mes jouets étaient passés. J'avais vingt-cinq ans lorsque je les ai revus en rendant visite à un ami, styliste de métier. Il en possédait quelques-uns et s'en servait pour décorer des appartements. Ce fut l'étincelle qui mit le feu aux poudres. Les couleurs vigoureuses et les formes des jouets me fascinaient et un sentiment de nostalgie envahit tout mon être. Depuis ce jour, je suis fou des jouets en fer-blanc.

J'ai trouvé le premier dans un vieux magasin de jouets. C'était une voiture de pompiers rouge, elle dormait dans un coin sous la poussière. Je l'ai payée 180 yen, à peine un demi-dollar. Ensuite, je me suis rendu presque tous les jours dans le magasin et j'ai acheté tout ce que je pouvais me procurer. J'étais quasi insatiable: plus ma collection prenait de l'ampleur, plus je voulais posséder de jouets. Il arriva ce qui devait arriver et, dix-huit mois plus tard, ma maison était envahie de la cave au grenier par les jouets en fer-blanc. Cela peut paraître bizarre, mais j'en suis amoureux. Quand je rentrais épuisé du travail et retrouvais mes Tin Toys, j'avais l'impression de revivre. D'ailleurs cela n'a pas changé.

J'étais parti faire du ski à Innsbruck en Autriche, et cela bien avant que se déclare ma passion pour les jouets. J'avais une chambre chez des particuliers et les murs de leur maison étaient encore garnis des anciens récipients dans lesquels on avait préparé les repas pendant des générations. J'ai compris ici combien ces gens appréciaient les objets de fabrication artisanale.

Contrairement aux Européens qui entretiennent les objets anciens, les meubles par exemple, et les lèguent à leurs enfants, les Japonais jettent tout et le respect de l'objet utilitaire leur est parfaitement inconnu. Je me sens responsable de chacun de mes jouets de fer-blanc, je suis donc dans la lignée des «gardiens» traditionnels.

Bien que les jouets en fer-blanc soient fabriqués en série, ils possèdent un caractère artisanal prononcé. Ils sont composés d'environ 200, parfois 300 pièces assemblées à la main. Pour une voiture en fer-blanc, il faut par exemple estamper séparément la carrosserie, les portes et le sigle du constructeur sur le capot, chaque détail, si minime soit-il, doit être moulé individuellement. Les jouets actuels en plastique n'ont plus cet aspect délicatement ciselé, ce genre de fabrication reviendrait beaucoup trop cher aujourd'hui, de plus il n'existe plus d'artisans formés spécialement à ce travail. Quand je tiens un de ces jouets dans ma main, je sens le savoir, l'amour et la méticulosité que ces artisans ont fait passer dans leur petite merveille en fer-blanc.

Les jouets en fer-blanc sont des témoignages historiques. Ils ont survécu aux guerres et aux périodes de crise et nous parlent des modes, des couleurs et des préférences de leur époque. Vingt-deux années ont passé, et ils n'ont pas cessé de me fasciner.

Quand ma collection de jouets a dépassé les 10.000 pièces, je l'ai mise à la disposition de la télévision qui réalisait un message publicitaire pour un grand magasin. Le thème: la nuit est noire et calme, tout le monde dort. Soudain, les jouets s'animent et font la fête. Un peu avant le lever du soleil, ils retournent à leur place et se figent, comme si rien ne s'était passé. Ce film publicitaire a reçu un prix au festival de Cannes.

Le public a ainsi fait connaissance de ma collection qui a ensuite fait l'objet de nombreuses expositions. L'une d'elles a attiré plus de 36.000 visiteurs en quinze jours. Ce chiffre élevé m'a surpris et incité, il y a douze ans de cela, à fonder un musée qui donnerait l'occasion à de nombreuses personnes d'apprécier la magie des jouets en fer-blanc.

En avril 1986, le premier Toys Club-Museum a ouvert ses portes à Yokohama, d'autres ont suivi dans les années suivantes et je nourris maintenant le projet d'ouvrir mon septième musée, le «Antique Toy World Museum». On pourra y admirer des «Character Dolls» – des personnages en fer-blanc créés à l'image de Popeye, de Charlie Chaplin et de créations de Walt Disney – ce sera un gigantesque pays des merveilles réservé aux jouets. J'ai également organisé des expositions hors du Japon, à Los Angeles et San Francisco. En outre, des albums de photographies commentant l'histoire des jouets en fer-blanc ont été réalisés.

Trouver de belles pièces anciennes n'est plus chose facile aujourd'hui, mon bonheur n'en est que plus grand, et mon cœur bat la chamade, quand je découvre un jouet rare. Je crois que beaucoup de gens collectionnent des objets parce qu'ils veulent de cette manière agrandir sans cesse l'univers qu'ils se sont découvert. Je n'ai moi-même pas seulement complété ma collection, j'ai fait aussi au cours de toutes ces années la connaissance de nombreuses personnes et les rencontres les plus intéressantes.

Le destin des jouets est souvent triste: on les jette, on les oublie sur le terrain de jeux; d'autres, les invendables, finissent sur le tas d'ordures où le marchand les a amenés. Si je les trouve sur mon chemin, je les emmène chez moi et les nettoie, j'ôte la saleté et la rouille. Ensuite je les graisse et les polis avec soin: lorsqu'ils ont retrouvé leur brillance, les jouets semblent revivre. Un bout de tôle laissé pour compte s'est métamorphosé en antiquité.

Cela fait vingt-deux ans que je collectionne ces jouets et je vais continuer à les sauver et à les conserver dans mes musées, pour faire connaître au public la beauté des jouets en fer-blanc. Je suis persuadé que telle est ma mission, et il n'existe rien de plus beau pour moi que de voir des gens regarder ma collection et découvrir le charme des Tin Toys.

Boats, Planes & Trains

1880s, *Locomotive*, unknown, 162 x 36 x 50 mm

1900s, *Biplane*, unknown, 180 x 140 x 90 mm

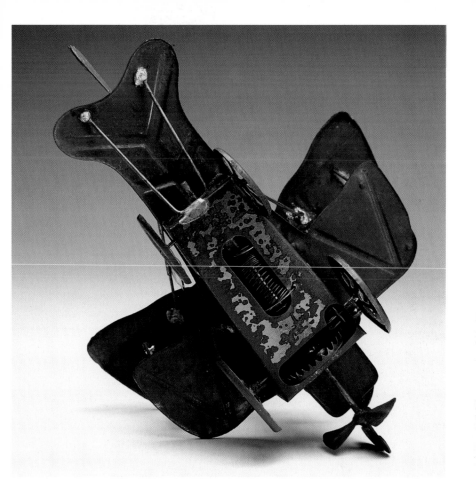

1930s, *Locomotive*, Y. M. Toy, 370 x 85 x 130 mm

1910s, *Locomotive*, unknown, 140 x 60 x 65 mm

1910s, *Airship*, unknown, 170 x 75 x 110 mm

1910s, *Streetcar*, unknown, 150 x 150 x 160 mm

1930s, *Streetcar*, unknown, 175 x 175 x 100 mm

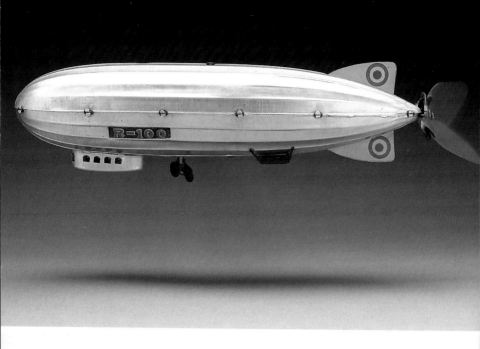

1920s, *Airship*, Kohno Kakuzo, 315 x 70 x 77 mm

1920s, *Airship*, Kohno Kakuzo, 430 x 65 x 75 mm

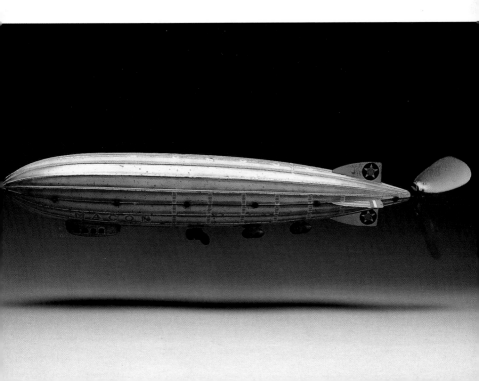

1930s, *Aikoku*, Tomiyama, 185 x 185 x 110 mm

1920s, *Biplane*, Toyodo, 155 x 125 x 100 mm

1920s, *Boat*, unknown, 230 x 55 x 100 mm

1920s, *Merry-Go-Round Planes*, unknown, 230 x 230 x 260 mm

1920s, *Merry-Go-Round Planes*, unknown, 180 x 180 x 230 mm

1920s, *Streetcar*, Saito, 330 x 55 x 90 mm

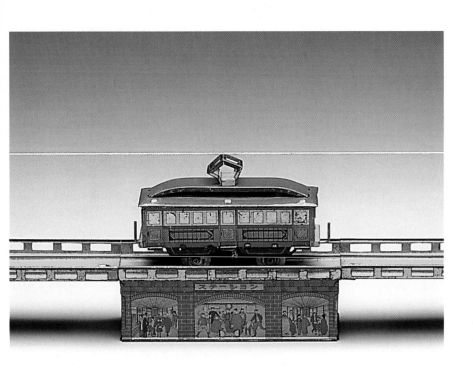

1930s, *Streetcar*, Kuramochi, 870 x 50 x 125 mm

▲1950s, *Boy & Duck Boat*, Hewa Toy, 185 x 80 x 100 mm

1930s, *Electric Locomotive*, unknown, 345 x 150 x 85 mm

1930s, *Diesel Engine Car*, A. K. Toy, 450 x 65 x 75 mm

1930s, *Streetcar*, Masudaya, 100 x 360 x 80 mm

1930s, *Streetcar*, Masudaya, 95 x 300 x 80 mm

1950s, *Streetcar*, Nomura, 150 x 60 x 85 mm

1960s, *Traction Engine*, Sankei, 195 x 100 x 150 mm

▲ 1950s, *Airplane*, Nikko Gangukogyo, 165 x 180 x 80 mm

1950s, *Seaplane*, Yonezawa, 125 x 135 x 85 mm

1950s, *Clipper*, Yonezawa, 220 x 295 x 95 mm

1910s, *Queen Elizabeth*, Yonezawa, 410 x 100 x 115 mm

1950s, *B-36*, Tomiyama, 490 x 660 x 155 mm

1950s, *Submarine*, Marusan, 190 x 40 x 50 mm

1950s, *Submarine*, Marusan, 325 x 55 x 100 mm

1930s, *Ferry*, Kuramochi, 260 x 110 x 150 mm

1940s, *Showboat*, unknown, 225 x 140 x 120 mm

1950s, *China Clipper*, Wyandotte Toys, 280 x 320 x 130 mm

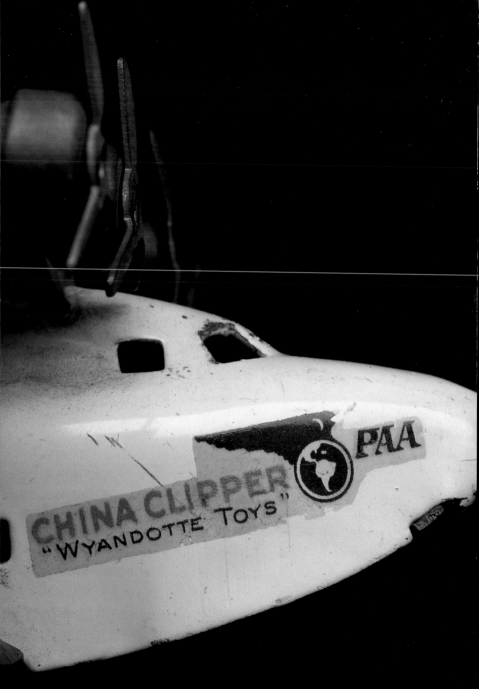

1950s, *UR-46 Helicopter*, Masudaya, 260 x 220 x 125 mm

1950s, *Rescue Helicopter*, Marusan, 210 x 220 x 100 mm

1950s, *Row-boat*, Momoya, 200 x 95 x 105 mm

1950s, *Racing Boat*, Tomiyama, 238 x 90 x 82 mm

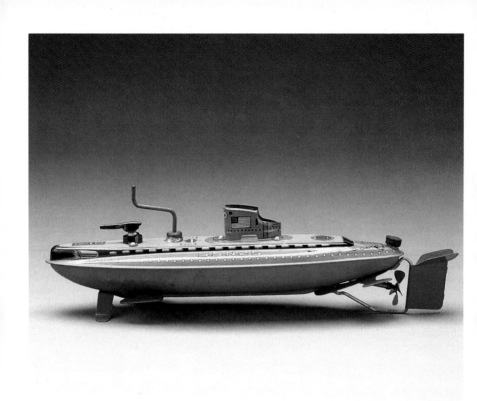

1950s, *Submarine*, Marusan, 255 x 55 x 70 mm

1950s, *Moby Dick*, Line Mar, 295 x 80 x 100 mm

1950s, *Locomotive*, Yonezawa, 290 x 75 x 120 mm

1950s, *Stratocruiser*, Nikko Gangu, 290 x 360 x 135 mm

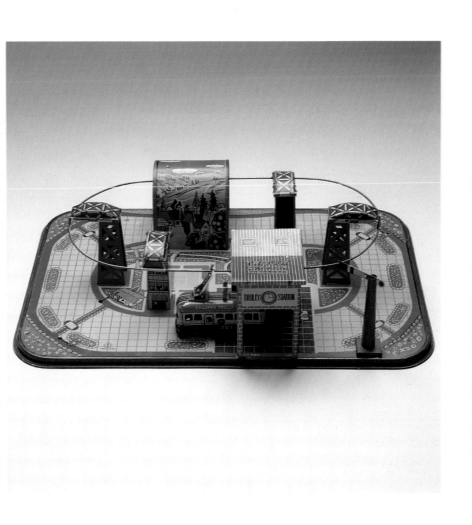

1950s, *Trolley Bus*, Yonezawa, 280 x 430 x 100 mm

1950s, *Locomotive*, Tomiyama, 230 x 60 x 110 mm

1950s, *Streetcar*, Asakusa Gangu Ningyo, Yonezawa, 335 x 65 x 125 mm

1950s, *San Francisco Streetcar*, Alps, 245 x 78 x 115 mm

1950s, *Streetcar*, Yoshiya, 250 x 60 x 145 mm

1950s, *Queen of the Sea*, Masudaya, 545 x 110 x 170 mm

1960s, *Airplane*, Yonezawa, 360 x 285 x 110 mm

1950s, *Airplane*, unknown, 230 x 320 x 80 mm

1950s, *Boeing Stratocruiser*, Nikko Gangu, 420 x 520 x 165 mm

1950s, *Pan American*, Nikko Gangu, 290 x 360 x 135 mm

1950s, *Pan American*, Gama, 370 x 505 x 180 mm

1950s, *Douglas DC-7*, Nomura, 315 x 430 x 110 mm

1930s, *TWA*, unknown, 290 x 390 x 105 mm

1950s, *Passenger Plane*, U.S.A., 555 x 690 x 140 mm

1950s, *DC-7 United*, Nomura, 450 x 490 x 150 mm

Robots & Spaceships

◀ 1950s, *Robert Robot*, unknown, 160 x 180 x 345 mm

▲ 1950s, *Robot and Son*, Louis Marx, 150 x 185 x 365 mm

1970s, *Robots*, Hong Kong, 98 x 140 x 280 mm

1950s, *Space Station*, Waco, 150 x 445 x 380 mm

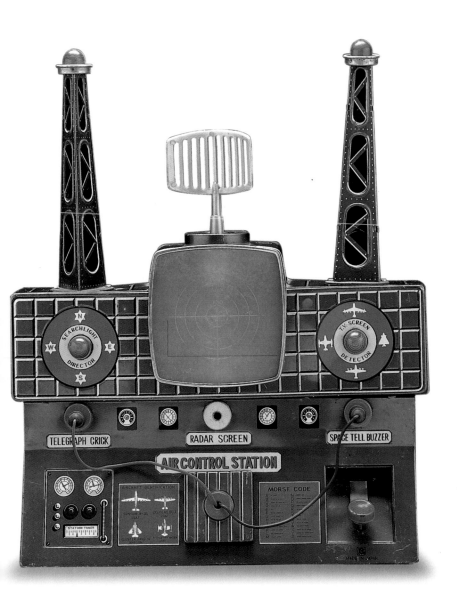

1950s, *Air Control Station*, unknown

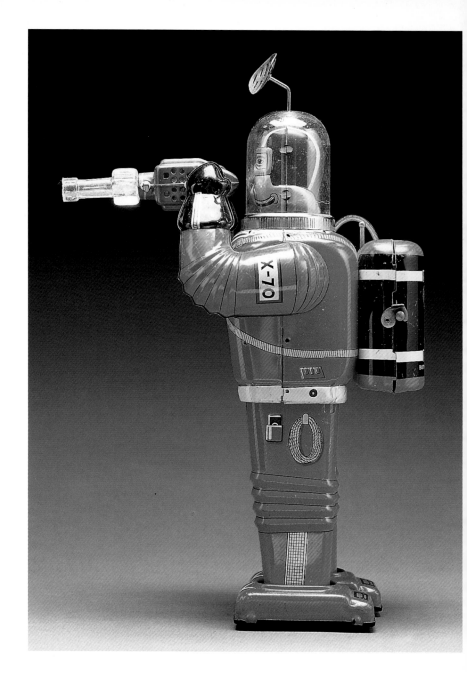

1950s, *Astronaut*, Daiya, 137 x 110 x 298 mm

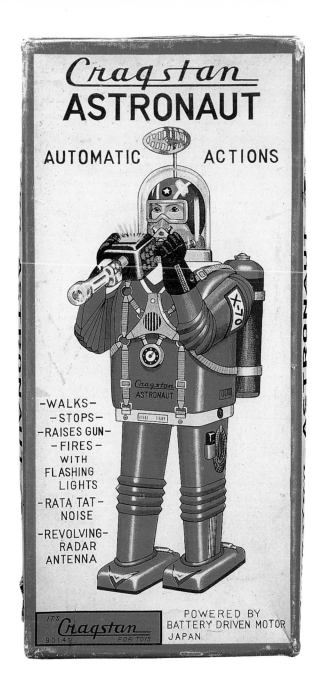

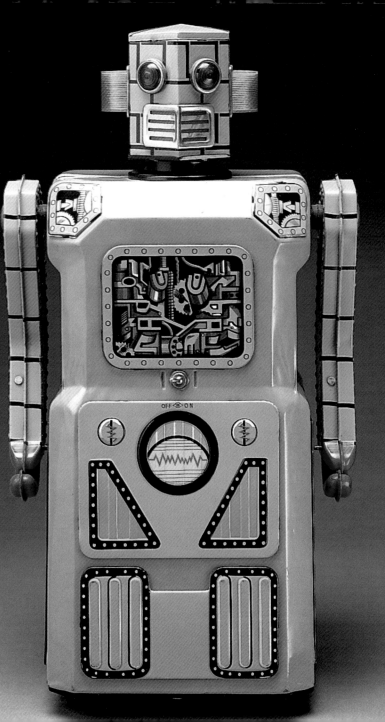

1950s, *Nonstop Robot*, Masudaya, 155 x 210 x 370 mm

1950s, *Robots*, Yonezawa, 52 x 70 x 150 mm

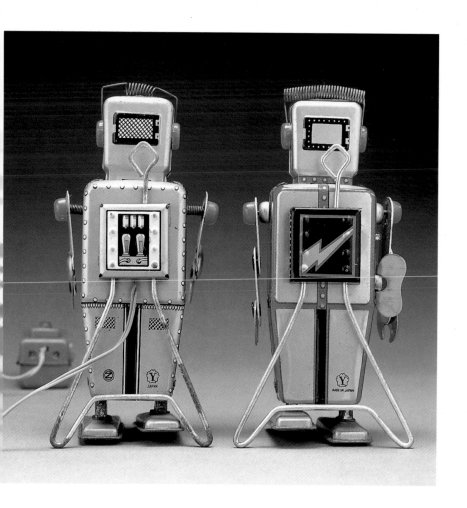

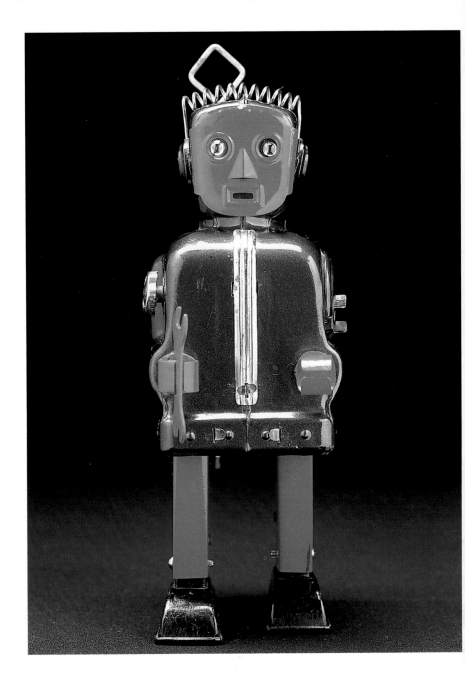

1950s, *Zoomer the Robot*, Nomura, 100 x 70 x 190 mm

1950s, *Robot*, Yonezawa, 70 x 85 x 215 mm

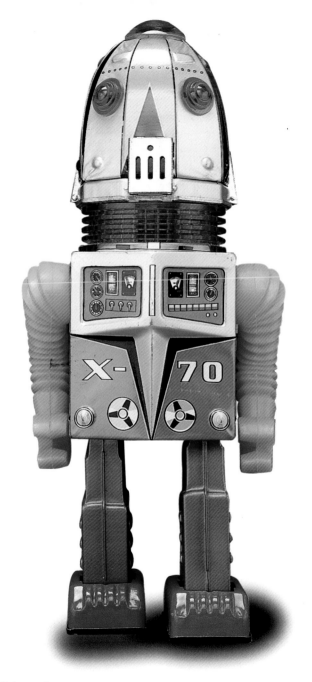

1960s, *X-70 Robot*, unknown, 90 x 130 x 305 mm

1950s, *Super-Bike*, Bandai, 305 x 70 x 138 mm

1950s, *Space Tank*, unknown, 203 x 118 x 105 mm

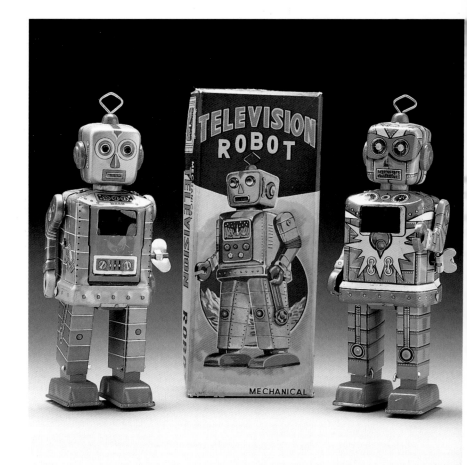

1950s, *Television Robots and Case*, Sankei, 65 x 80 x 198 mm

1950s, *Sparky Robots*, SY Toys, 56 x 80 x 190, 56 x 180 x 175, 56 x 80 x 175 mm

▲ 1950s, *Space Explorer*, Yonezawa, 70 x 120 x 230 mm

▲ 1950s, *Zoomer the Robot*, Nomura, 100 x 70 x 190 mm

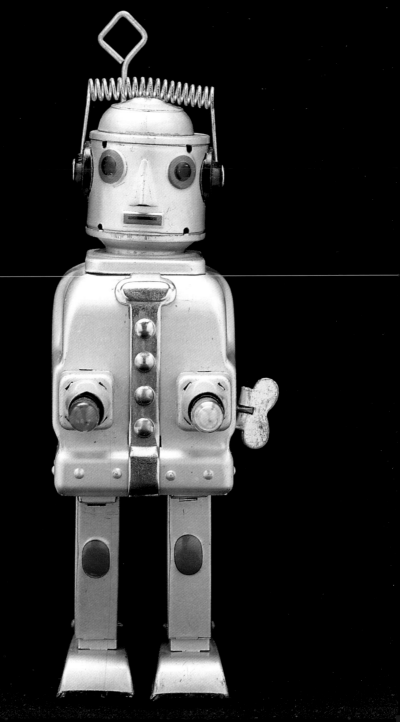

1950s, *Satellite*, Masudaya, 200 x 200 x 110 mm

1950s *Thunder Robot*, Asakusa Toy, 90 x 160 x 285 mm

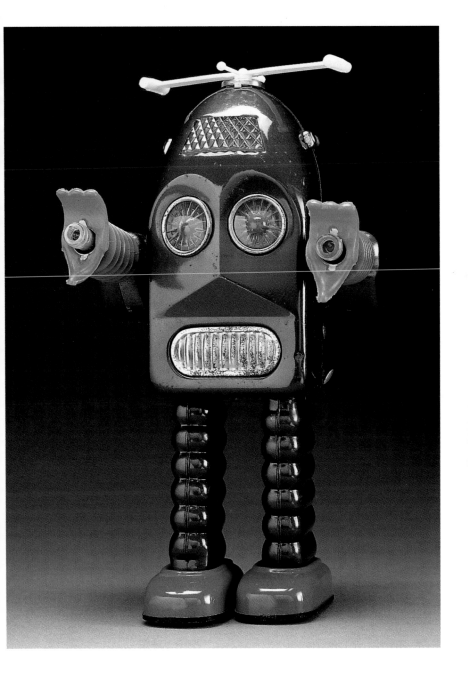

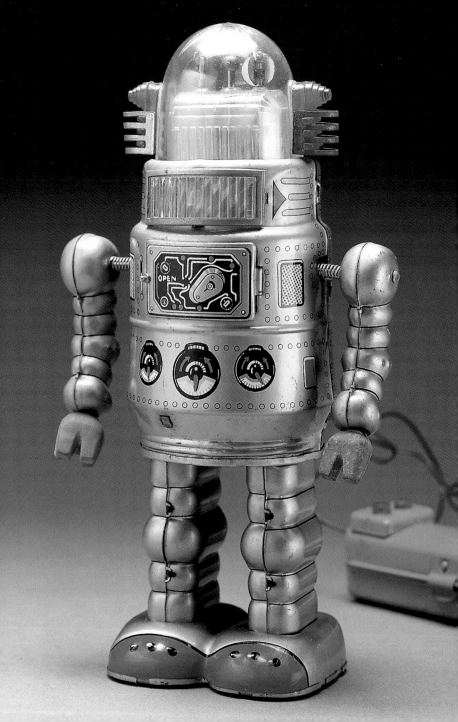

1950s, *Robot*, unknown, 75 x 125 x 230 mm

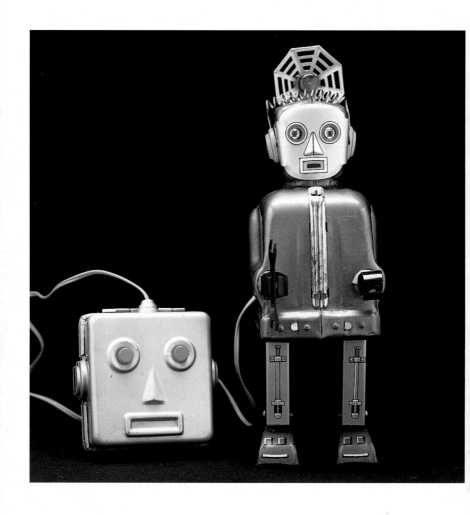

▲ 1950s, *Radar Robot*, Nomura, 100 x 70 x 225 mm

OFF - ON

1950s, *Sonicon Rocket*, Masudaya, 340 x 170 x 230 mm

1950s, *Sonicon Rocket*, Masudaya, 340 x 170 x 230 mm

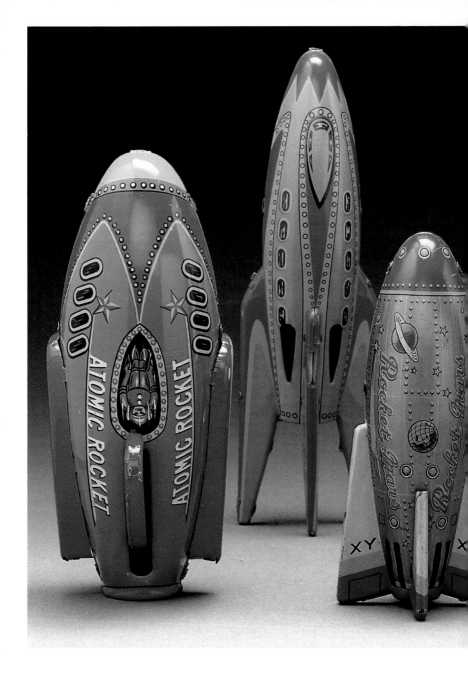

1950s, *Various Rockets, different sizes*

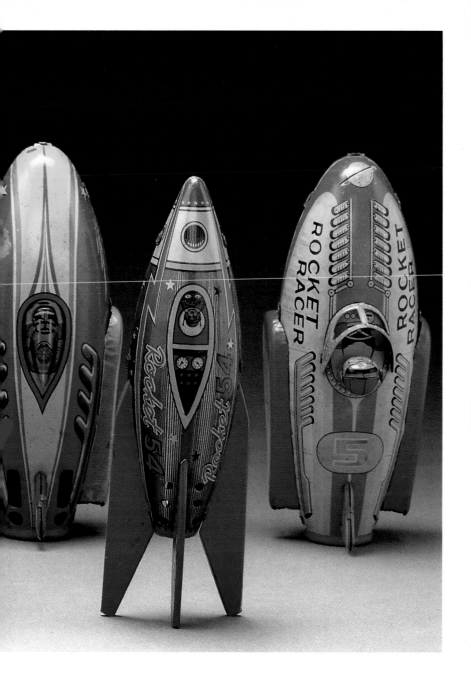

1950s, *Rocket No. 3*, Masudaya, 165 x 70 x 60 mm

1950s, *Atomic Rocket*, Masudaya, 170 x 70 x 72 mm

1950s, *Space Robot*, Asahi Toy, 127 x 127 x 80 mm

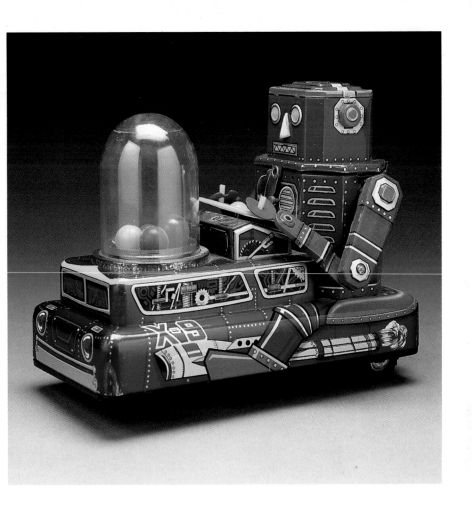

1950s, *X-9 Robot*, Masudaya, 190 x 115 x 155 mm

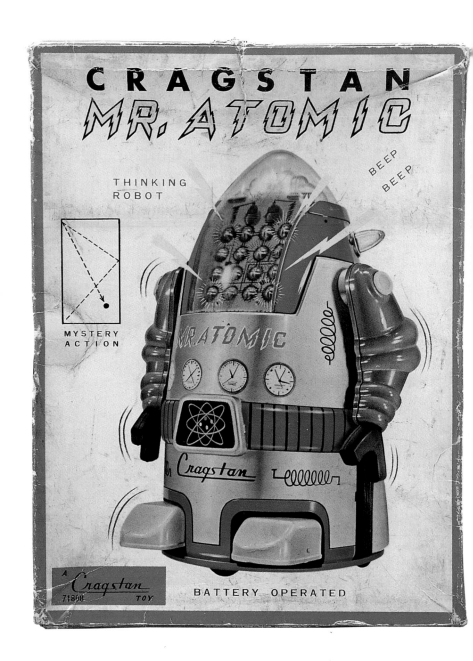

1950s, *Mr. Atomic*, Yonezawa, 155 x 175 x 225 mm

▲1950s, *Robot*, Line Mar, 55 x 110 x 165 mm

▲1950s, *Smoking Robot*, Yonezawa, 105 x 160 x 300 mm

1960s, *Satellite X-107*, Masudaya, 200 x 200 x 128 mm

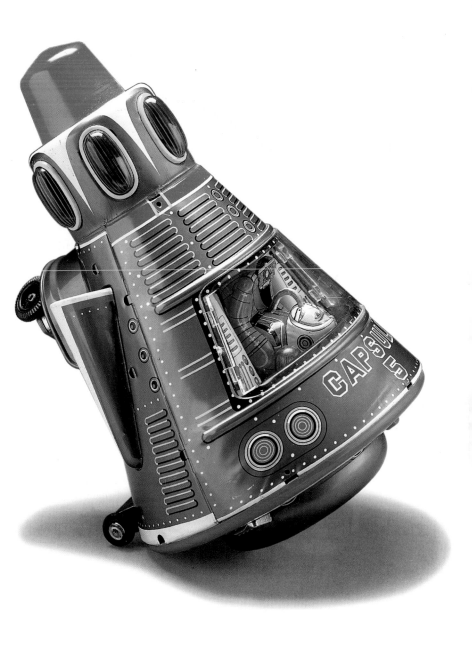

1950s, *Capsule 5*, Masudaya, 265 x 160 x 175 mm

1950s, *Astro Scout*, Yonezawa, 85 x 130 x 230 mm

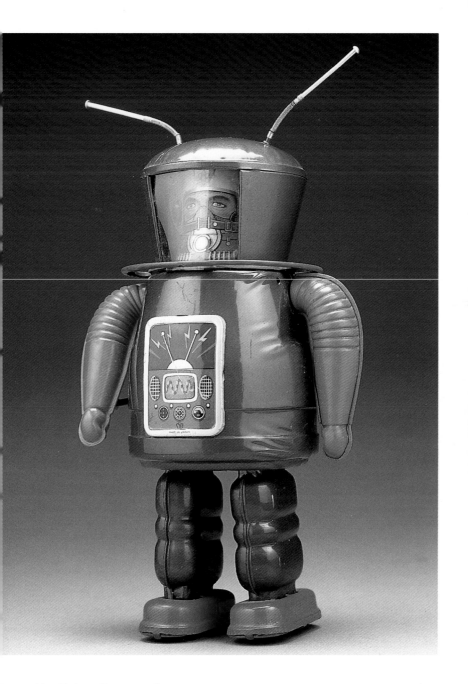

1950s, *X-27 Explorer*, Yonezawa, 85 x 125 x 213 mm

1960s, *Space Frontier*, Yoshino Toy, 445 x 120 x 215 mm

1950s, *Space Patrol*, Ohta, 180 x 63 x 110 mm

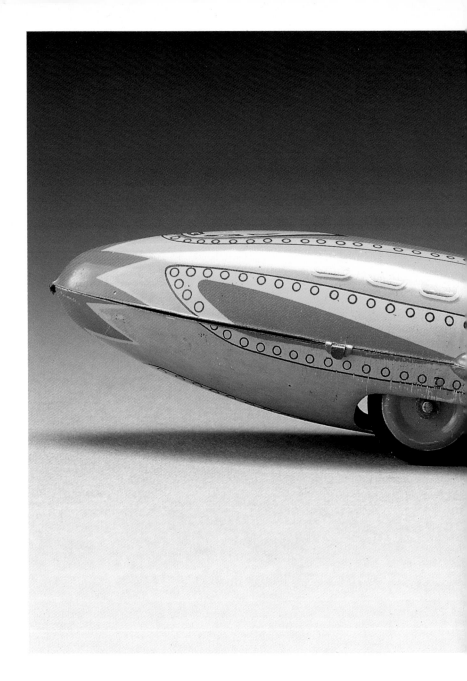

1950s, *Space Ship X-3*, Masudaya, 205 x 62 x 47 mm

1950s, *Robot Tractor*, Showa, 250 x 125 x 150 mm

1950s, *Robot Bulldozer*, Yoshiya, 180 x 97 x 120 mm

▲ 1950s, *Robots*, Yonezawa, 115 x 155 x 275 mm

◄1960s, *Wheel Robot*, Asahi, 120 x 95 x 170 mm

▲1960s, *Seesaw Robot*, Yonezawa, 160 x 65 x 150 mm

1960s, *TV Robots*, Horikawa, 110 x 136 x 325 mm

1950s, 1960s, *Gear Robots*, unknown, Horikawa, 82 x 138 x 282 mm

1950s, *Space Tank*, Yoshiya, 150 x 90 x 107 mm

▲1950s, *Atomic X-8*, Mitsuhashi, 145 x 80 x 55 mm

1950s, *Elephant Robot*, Yoshiya, 130 x 90 x 120 mm

1950s, *Space Dog*, Yoshiya, 185 x 75 x 115 mm

1950s, *Space Robot*, Yonezawa, 240 x 120 x 135 mm

1960s, *Moon Scout*, Louis Marx, 90 x 160 x 290 mm

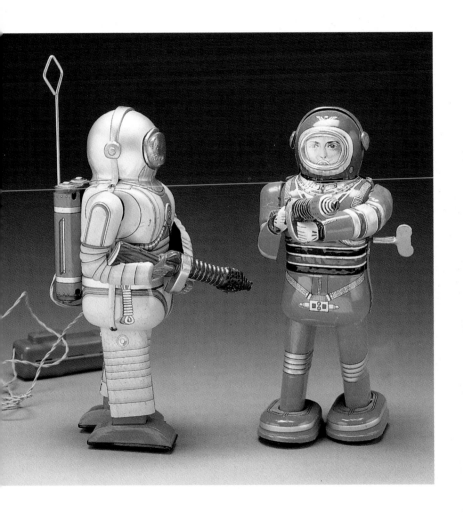

1950s, *Astronauts*, Nomura, Daiya, 75 x 95 x 230 mm

▲ 1960s, *Space Man, Space Commander*, Horikawa, 95 x 140 x 280, 120 x 140 x 260 mm

1950s, *Robby*, Yoshiya, 65 x 92 x 160 mm

1950s, *Robby*, Nomura, 95 x 125 x 215 mm

1950s, *Robby*, Nomura, 135 x 175 x 310 mm

1960s, *Moon Rocket*, Masudaya, 235 x 112 x 170 mm

1950s, *Robby Space Patrol*, Nomura, 330 x 150 x 225 mm

◄ 1960s, *Moon Explorer*, Yonezawa, 200 x 130 x 180 mm

▲ 1950s, *Capsule 6*, Masudaya, 255 x 120 x 130 mm

1950s, *Rocket Mars*, Cragstan, 140 x 62 x 47 mm

1950s, *Rocket 54*, unknown, 168 x 58 x 45 mm

▲ 1950s, *Rocket Racer*, Masudaya, 165 x 70 x 75 mm

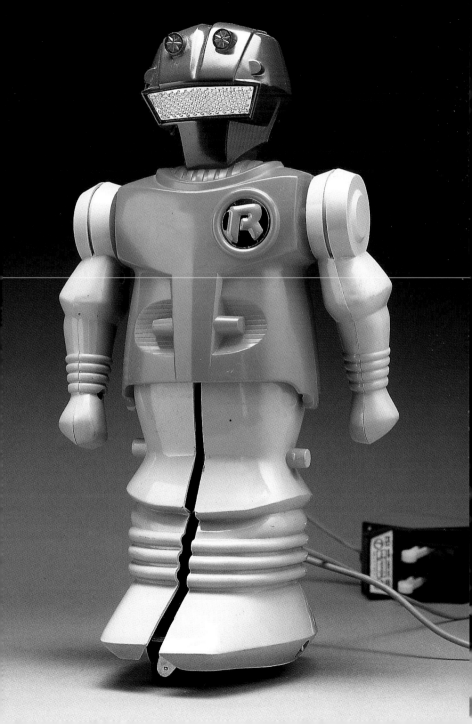

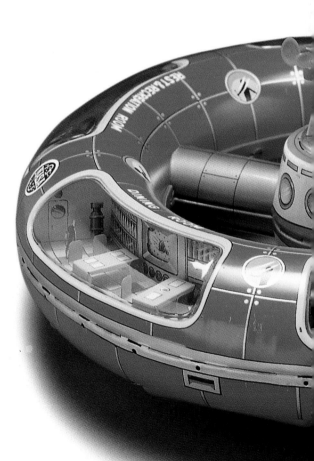

1950s, *Space Station*, Horikawa, 300 x 300 x 230 mm

1950s, *Moon Robot*, Yonezawa, 110 x 125 x 260 mm

1950s, *Astronaut*, Yonezawa, 95 x 125 x 240 mm

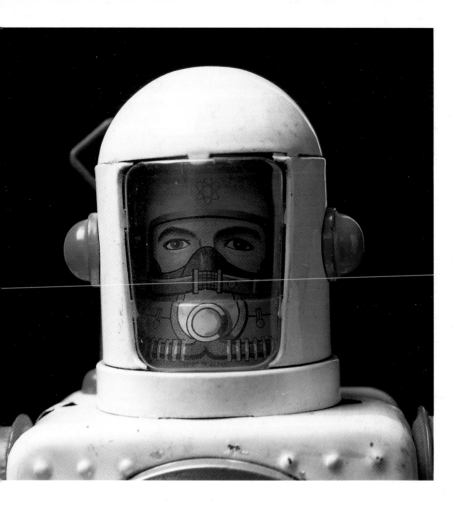

1950s, *Space Scout*, Yonezawa, 100 x 115 x 240 mm

1950s, *Space Man*, Yoshiya, 65 x 75 x 215 mm

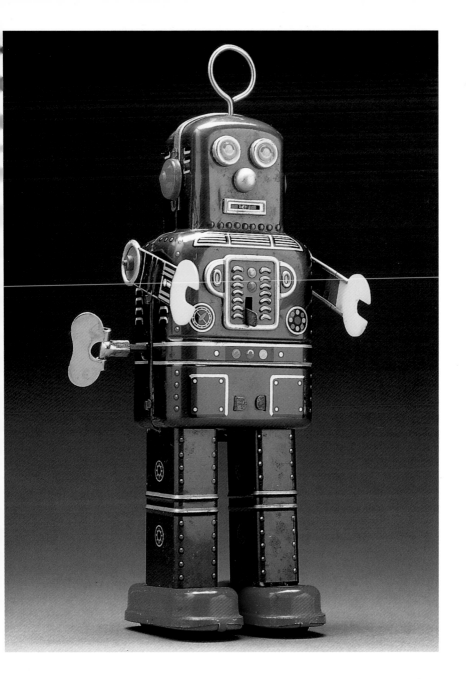

◀ 1960s, *Spacecraft*, Kanto Toy, 160 x 95 x 110 mm

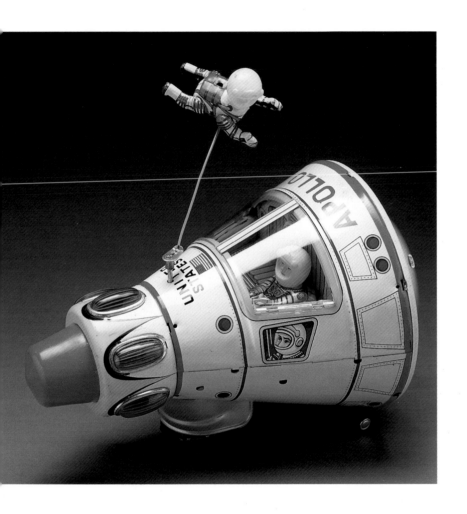

▲ 1960s, *Apollo Spacecraft*, Masudaya, 265 x 170 x 240 mm

1960s, *Fire Bird*, Masudaya, 340 x 170 x 130 mm

1960s, *Moon Explorer*, Masudaya, 340 x 170 x 130 mm

1960s, *Space Tank*, Masudaya, 215 x 105 x 200 mm

1960s, *Space Patrol*, unknown, 150 x 90 x 95 mm

1950s, *Space Explorer*, Yonezawa, 92 x 110 x 290 mm

BATTERY OPERATED

SPACE EXPLORER

NO. 802 MADE IN JAPAN

1950s, *Tremendous Mikes*, Aoshin, 90 x 155 x 260 mm

1950s, *Diamond Planet Robots*, Yonezawa, 140 x 200 x 260 mm

1950s, *Sky Express*, Usagiya, 218 x 58 x 60 mm

1950s, *Robot with Lantern*, Line Mar, 90 x 115 x 200 mm

1950s, *Robot*, Masudaya, 65 x 110 x 190 mm

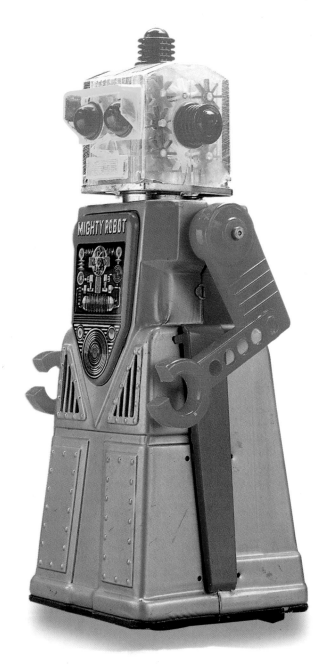

1960s, *Mighty Robot*, Yoshiya, 110 x 150 x 300 mm

1950s, *Ranger Robot*, Daiya, 115 x 110 x 265 mm

▲ 1950s, *Tetsujin 28-GO*, Miura, 112 x 78 x 118 mm

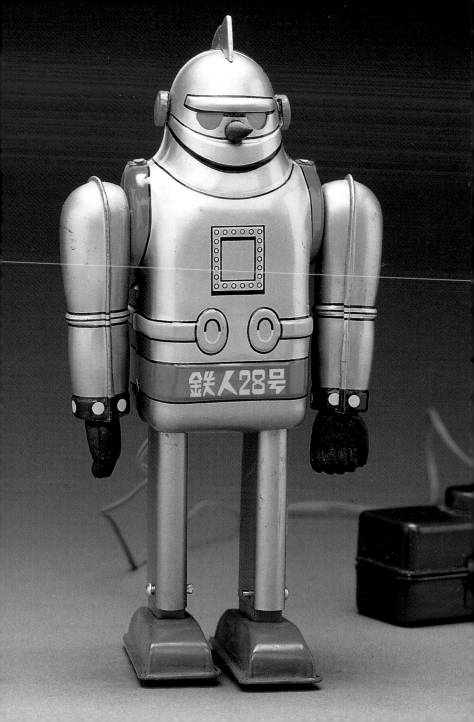

1960s, *Robots*, unknown, 82 x 105 x 220 mm

1950s, 1960s, *Astronauts,* SY Toys, Shudo, 50 x 90 x 145, 45 x 85 x 128 mm

1950s, *Giant Robot*, Horikawa, 148 x 220 x 400 mm

1960s, *Talking Robot*, Yonezawa, 112 x 150 x 275 mm

1960s, *Atomic Robot and Case*, Yonezawa, 55 x 140 x 160 mm

1950s, *Space Man and Case*, SY Toys, 64 x 80 x 195 mm

1960s, *Tetsujin 28-GO*, Bandai, 220 x 115 x 168 mm

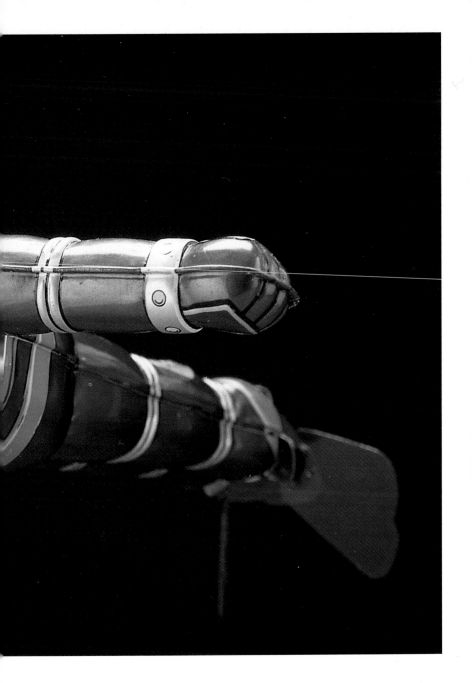

◄ 1960s, *Ultra Man*, Bull Mark, 90 x 150 x 320 mm

▲ 1960s, *Mirror Man, Ultra Man, Ultra 7*, Bull Mark, 50 x 100 x 235 mm

1960s, *U-5 Robot*, Daiya, 83 x 105 x 193 mm

1960s, *Hysterical Robot*, unknown, 165 x 160 x 340 mm

1960s, *Robotank R-1*, Nomura, 195 x 140 x 260 mm

1960s, *Robotank-Z*, Nomura, 195 x 140 x 260 mm

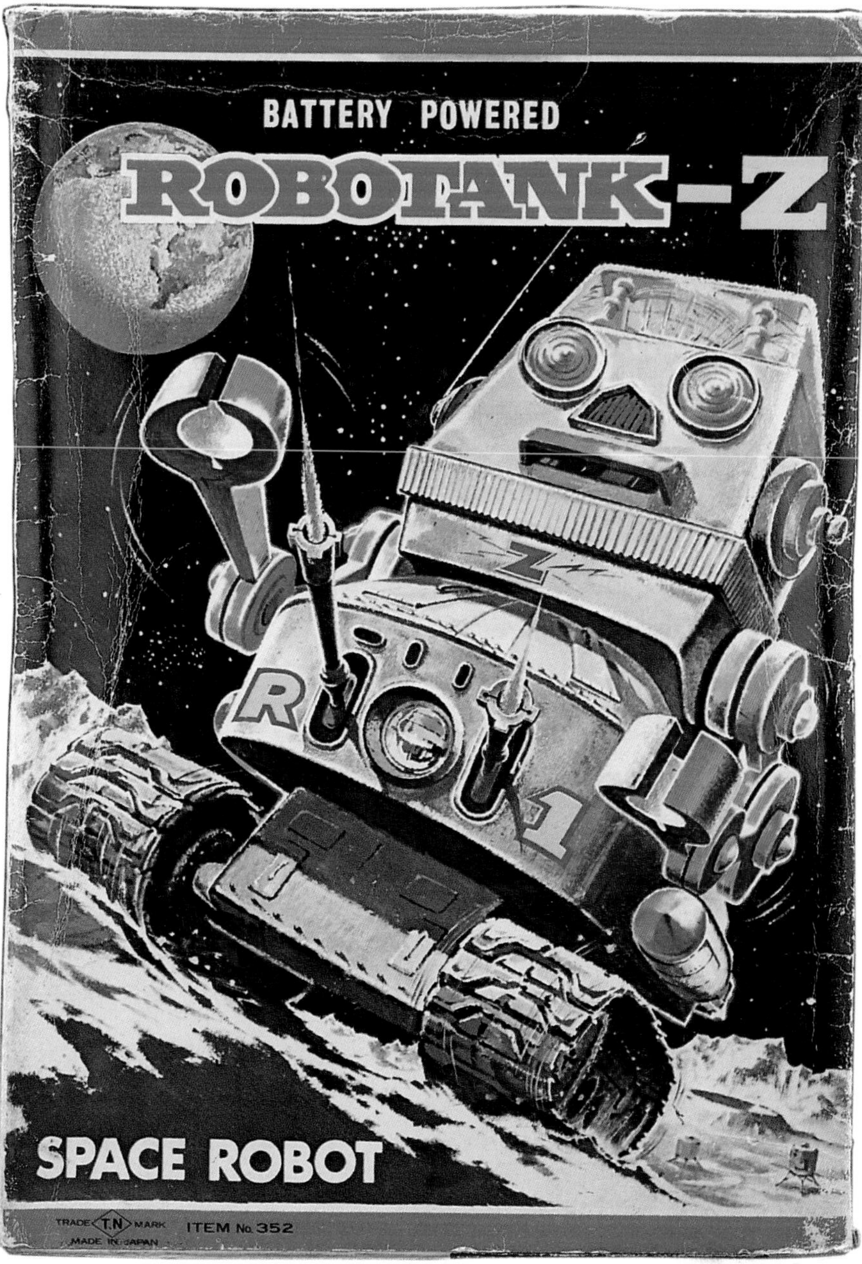

BATTERY POWERED

ROBOTANK - Z

SPACE ROBOT

TRADE **T.N** MARK   ITEM No. 352
MADE IN JAPAN

1960s, *Tetsujin 28-GO*, unknown, 273 x 138 x 150 mm

▲ 1960s, *RT-8 Robot, Robot*, Nomura, unknown, 95 x 73 x 120, 80 x 95 x 135 mm

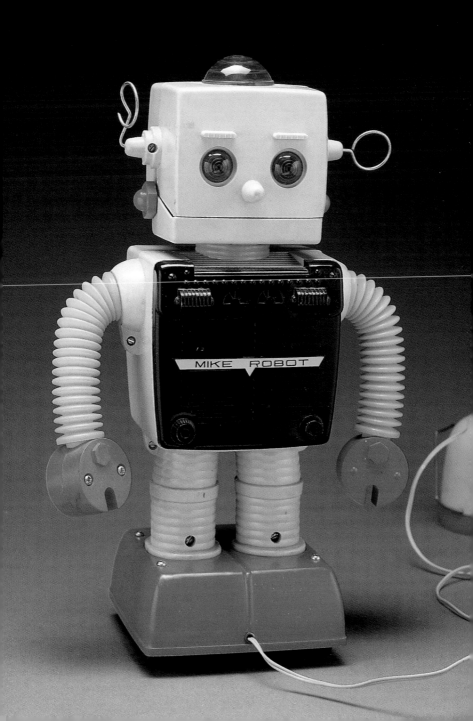

1960s, *Gear Robots*, Horikawa, 65 x 115 x 210 mm

1960s, *Mars Explorers*, Horikawa, 105 x 120 x 240 mm

1960s, *Krome Dome*, Yonezawa, 130 x 130 x 260 mm

1960s, *Roto Robot*, Horikawa, 73 x 105 x 220 mm

1960s, *Moon Explorer*, Bandai, 107 x 165 x 452 mm

1970s, *Ultra Man Leo*, Bull Mark, 85 x 160 x 320 mm

1960s, *Ohgon Bat*, Nomura, 90 x 135 x 285 mm

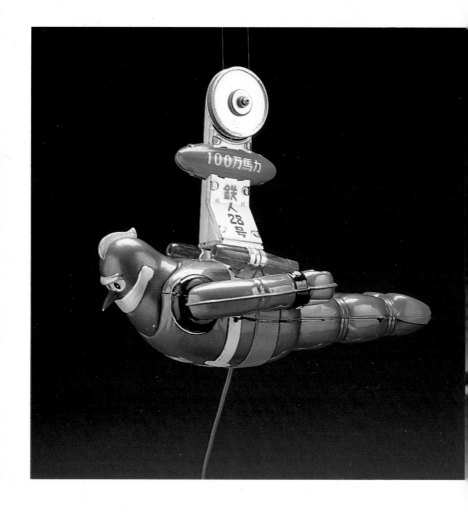

▲ 1960s, *Tetsujin 28-GO*, Nomura, 230 x 240 x 90 mm

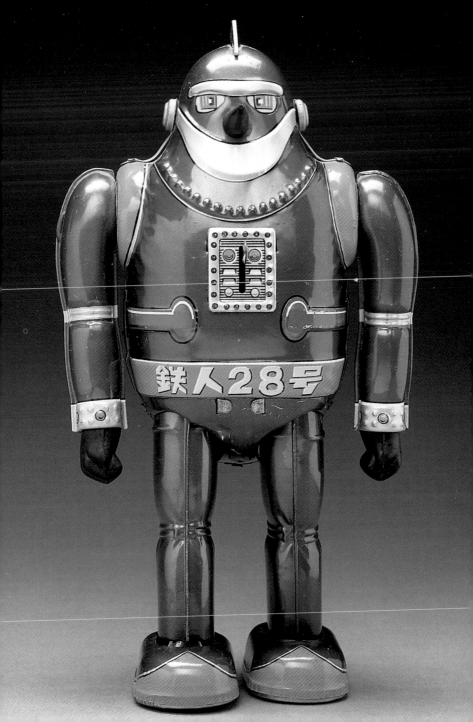

1960s, *Robots*, Horikawa, 100 x 140 x 290 mm

1960s, *Thunder Robots*, Horikawa, 90 x 135 x 285 mm

1960s, *Astro Man*, Nomura, 90 x 135 x 260 mm

1960s, *Astronaut*, Rosko Toy, 110 x 135 x 330 mm

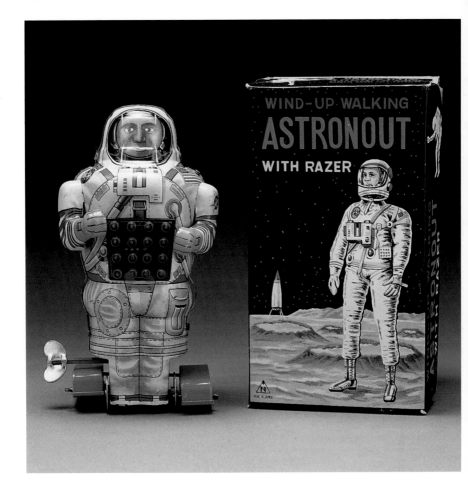

1970s, *Astronaut and Case*, unknown, 85 x 95 x 155 mm

1950s, *Sparking Robot and Case*, unknown, 75 x 115 x 160 mm

1960s, *Metamorph*, Marumiya, 100 x 160 x 335 mm

1960s, *Astronauts*, Daiya, 125 x 170 x 340 mm

▲1950s, *Smoking Robot*, Yonezawa, 105 x 160 x 300 mm

1960s, *Robots*, Horikawa, 105 x 140 x 290 mm

1960s, *Robots*, Horikawa, 87 x 135 x 280, 87 x 135 x 290 mm

1950s, *Space Tank*, Union, 157 x 90 x 115 mm

1960s, *Atom Robot and Case*, Yoshiya, 80 x 70 x 160 mm

◄ 1960s, *Acrobat*, Yonezawa, 70 x 100 x 245 mm

▲ 1960s, *Robot*, Yonezawa, 70 x 150 x 260 mm

1960s, *Mars Rocket*, Masudaya, 365 x 190 x 140 mm

1960s, *Metamorph*, Horikawa, 98 x 140 x 283 mm

1960s, *Tetsujin 28-GO Robots*, Nomura, 65 x 115 x 195 mm

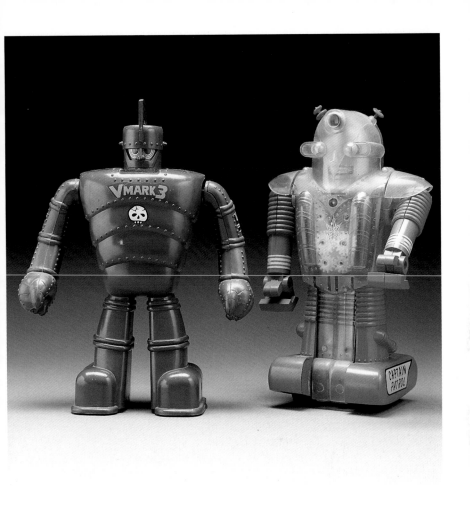

1960s, *V Mark 3*, *Captain Patrol*, unknown, Imai, 65 x 118 x 215, 85 x 85 x 215 mm

◄1960s, *Gear Robot*, Taiyo, 135 x 155 x 370 mm

▲1960s, *Gear Robots*, Yoshiya, 90 x 85 x 255 mm

1970s, *Robots*, Yone Toy, 80 x 55 x 85, 80 x 55 x 85, 185 x 55 x 85 mm

1950s, *Space Patrol*, *Space Tank*, unknown, 140 x 140 x 95, 157 x 90 x 115 mm

1960s, *Space Patrols*, Yoshiya, 190 x 190 x 120 mm

1960s, *Apollo-11 LM*, Daishin, 180 x 180 x 245, 135 x 135 x 183 mm

1960s, *Space Station*, Horikawa, 295 x 295 x 165 mm

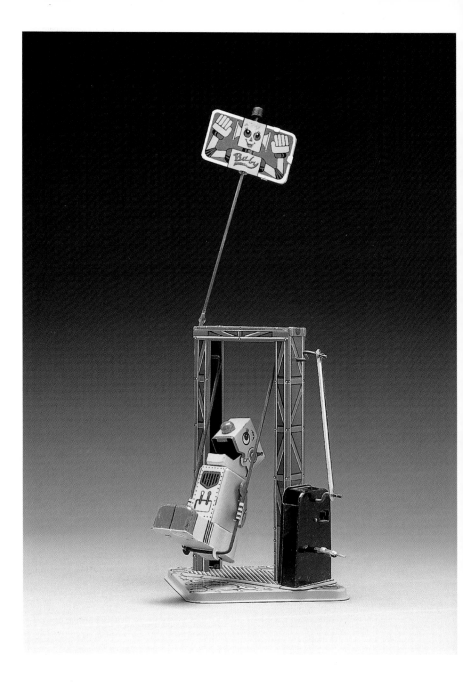

1960s, *Robot on Swing*, Yonezawa, 135 x 135 x 160 mm

1960s, *Robot on Swing*, Yonezawa, 135 x 135 x 160 mm

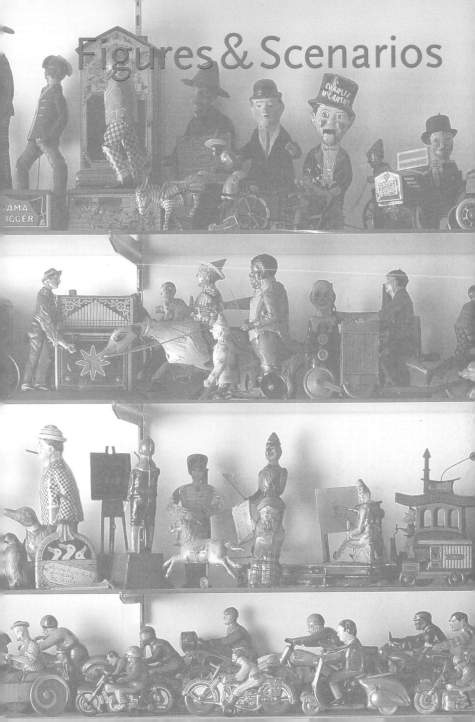

Figures & Scenarios

▲ 1900s, *Dutch Person Riding on Duck*, unknown, 95 x 45 x 85 mm

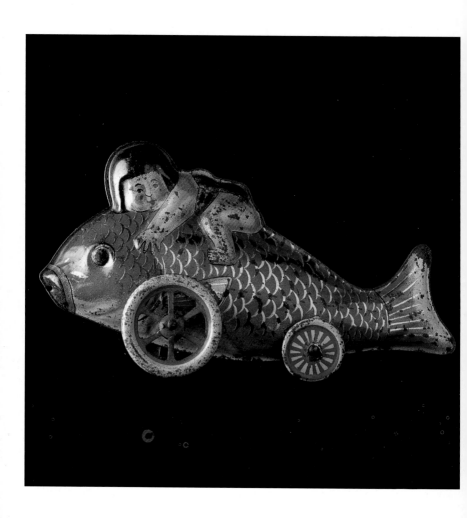

1910s, *Brave Kintaro*, unknown, 40 x 160 x 80 mm

1920s, *Horse and Carriage*, W.U. Toy, 225 x 80 x 140 mm

1910s, *Motor Tricycle*, unknown, 165 x 60 x 115 mm

1910s, *Pierrot and Riding Girl*, H. Yamada, 170 x 170 x 175 mm

1910s, *Rabbit*, unknown, 170 x 95 x 200 mm

◀ 1910s, *Doll Upon Drum*, Namiki, 120 x 60 x 220 mm

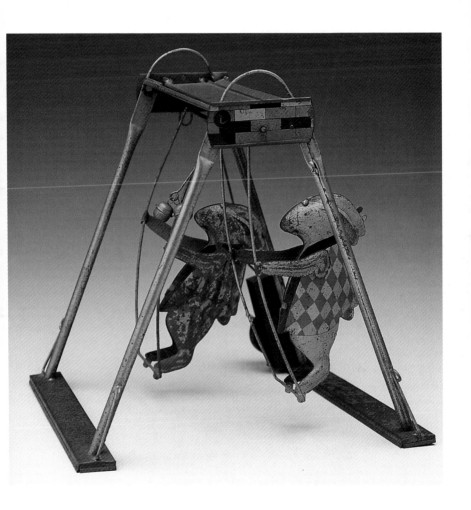

▲ 1910s, *Rabbits on Horizontal Bar*, unknown, 160 x 120 x 190 mm

1920s, *Grasshopper*, Y. Egawa, 180 x 90 x 80 mm

1920s, *Drummer*, unknown, 90 x 105 x 230 mm

1920s, *Ball Kicker*, Kuramochi, 220 x 60 x 140 mm

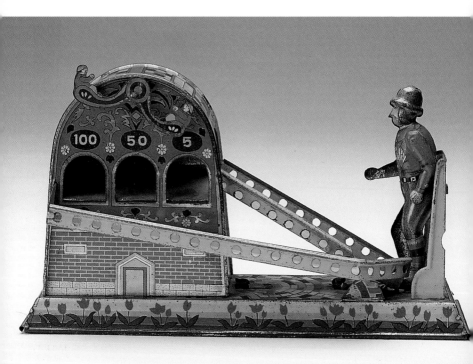

1920s, *Ball Kicker*, Kuramochi, 210 x 65 x 115 mm

1920s, *Hen Having a Meal*, Toyodo, 180 x 60 x 115 mm

1920s, *Rocking-horse Soldier*, unknown, 170 x 70 x 150 mm

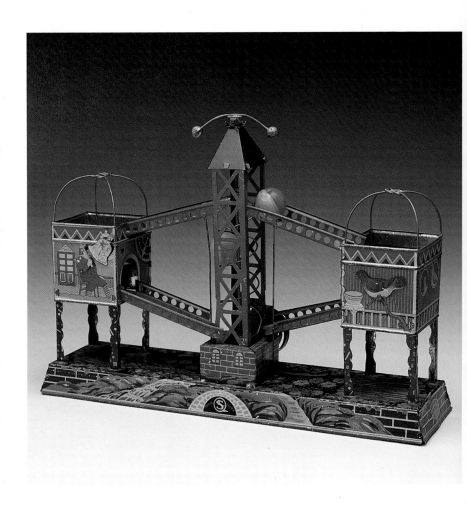

▲ 1920s, *Ball Escalator*, unknown, 80 x 310 x 220 mm

1920s, *Ball Escalator*, unknown, 190 x 130 x 220 mm

1920s, *Ball Escalator*, unknown, 135 x 135 x 230 mm

1920s, *Skier*, unknown, 135 x 70 x 95 mm

1920s, *Skiers*, unknown, 260 x 150 x 100 mm

1920s, *Ball Kicker*, unknown, 230 x 70 x 90 mm

1920s, *Merry Seesaw*, Kuramochi, 120 x 80 x 215 mm

1910s, *Windmill*, unknown, 145 x 75 x 170 mm

1920s, *Motor Bike*, Kuramochi, 200 x 200 x 120 mm

1920s, *Cat-and-Rat Wheelchair*, Kuramochi, 170 x 70 x 155 mm

1940s, *Witch Riding on Goose*, unknown, 240 x 80 x 190 mm

1920s, *Warrior Rocking-horse*, Ito, 180 x 55 x 145 mm

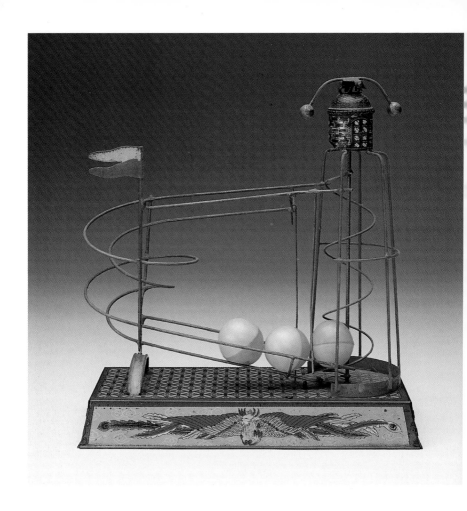

1920s, *Ball Escalator*, unknown, 85 x 200 x 210 mm

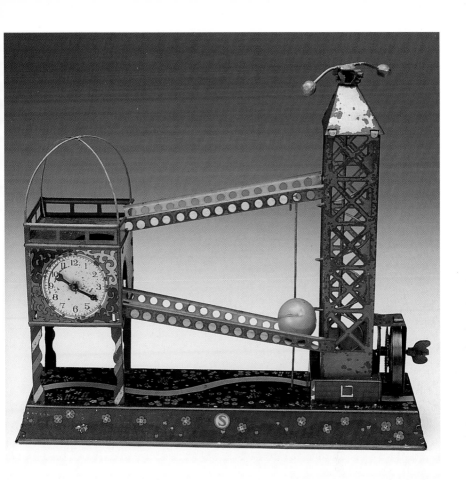

1920s, *Ball Escalator*, unknown, 65 x 240 x 210 mm

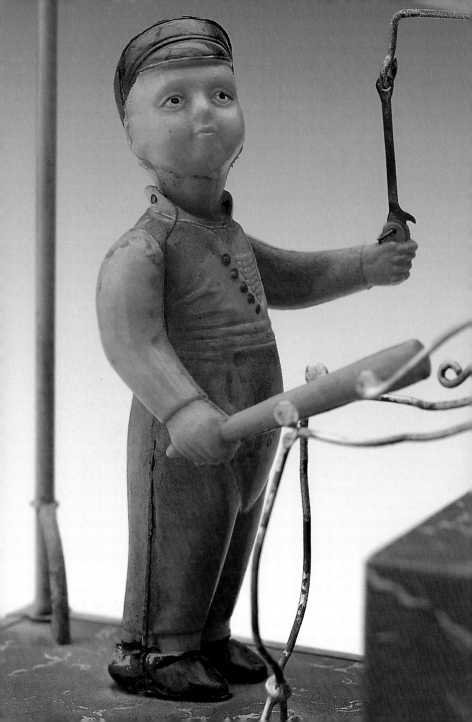

1920s, *Ball Game*, Chiba, 205 x 80 x 320 mm

1920s, *Horse-race*, H. Yamada, 85 x 280 x 100 mm

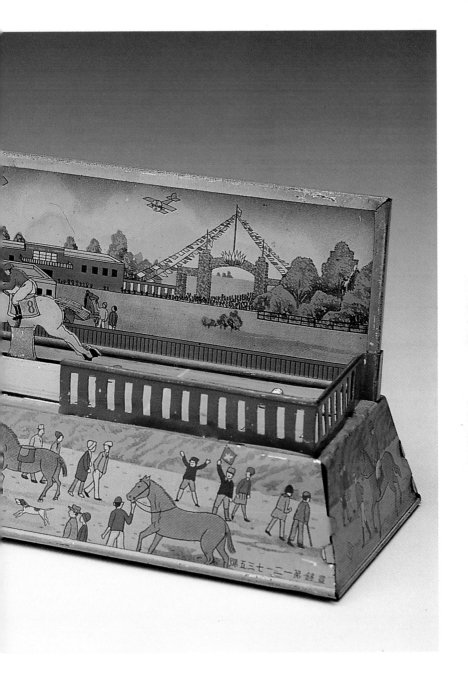

▲ 1930s, *Drummer, Banjo Player*, unknown, 155 x 120 x 240, 100 x 100 x 260 mm

1930s, *Children on Swing and Horizontal Bar*, unknown, 80 x 205 x 250 mm

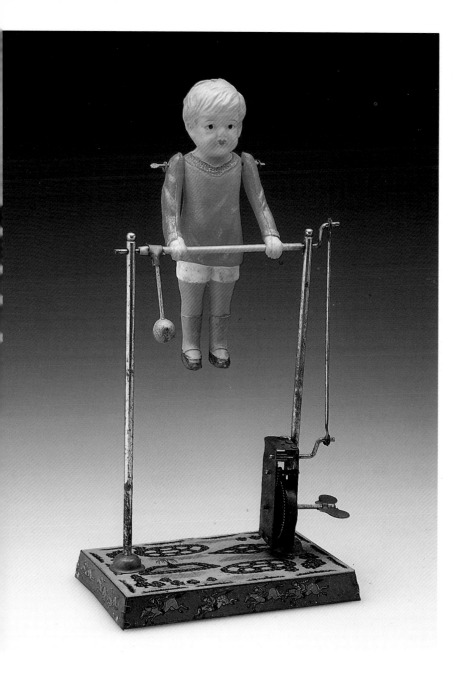

1930s, *Boy on Horizontal Bar*, Kuramochi, 90 x 140 x 205 mm

1930s, *Drummers*, unknown, 55 x 100 x 195 mm

1930s, *Foot Juggler*, Masudaya, 240 x 85 x 225 mm

◄1930s, *Boy with Stick*, unknown, 50 x 50 x 125 mm

▲1930s, *Dancing Couple*, unknown, 55 x 60 x 150 mm

1930s, *Girl Bouncing Ball*, unknown, 85 x 145 x 235 mm

1930s, *Boy Violinist*, unknown, 110 x 105 x 210 mm

1930s, *Dog*, C.C. Toy, 240 x 55 x 110 mm

1930s, *Dog*, Kuramochi, 100 x 50 x 80 mm

1930s, *Dancing Couple*, unknown, 115 x 115 x 200 mm

1940s, *Dancing Couple*, unknown, 60 x 60 x 125 mm

▲ 1930s, *Riding Warrior*, Masudaya, 210 x 70 x 175 mm

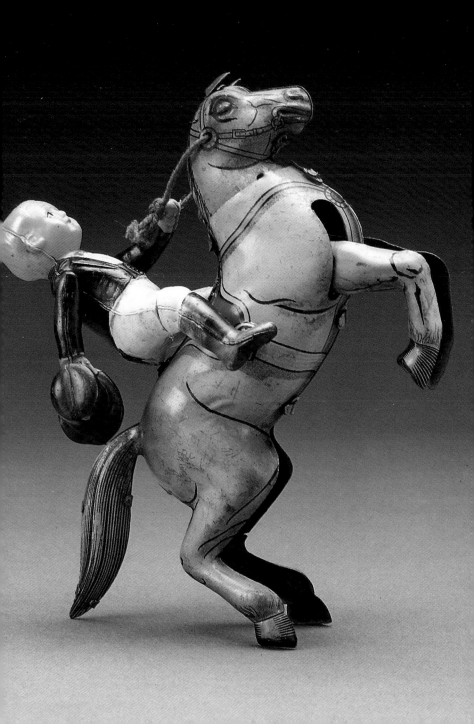

◄1930s, *Drummer-Boy*, Wakimura Company, 125 x 85 x 250 mm

▲1930s, *"Caterpillar" and Friends*, unknown, 190 x 55 x 90 mm

1950s, *Monkey with Xylophone*, unknown, 120 x 110 x 220 mm

1950s, *Monkey Artist*, unknown, 160 x 120 x 220 mm

▲ 1930s, *Figure sawing Logs*, Germany, 120 x 70 x 100 mm

1940s, *Figure sawing Logs*, Germany, 107 x 60 x 105 mm

1940s, *Worker*, Germany, 108 x 65 x 105 mm

▲ 1930s, *Two Elephants*, Kuramochi, 145 x 110 x 230 mm

1930s, *Pianist*, Yoshiya, 140 x 120 x 170 mm

1930s, *Happy Times*, Kuramochi, 120 x 170 x 225 mm

◄ 1930s, *Knife-Grinder*, Germany, 90 x 60 x 100 mm

▲ 1930s, *Knife-Grinder*, Germany, 170 x 80 x 135 mm

1930s, *Drummer-Boy*, R.F.Toy, 100 x 120 x 290 mm

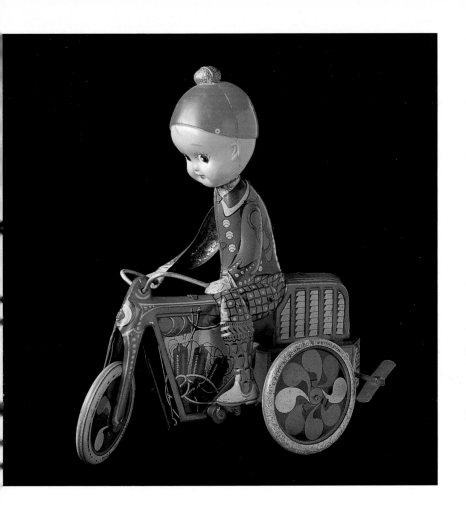

1930s, *Boy on Tricycle*, Wakimura Company, 195 x 85 x 205 mm

▲ 1930s, *Worker*, Germany, 100 x 70 x 110 mm

1930s, *Rabbit Violinist*, Kuramochi, 100 x 70 x 230 mm

1930s, *Rabbit Drummer*, Masudaya, 120 x 80 x 220 mm

◀ 1930s, *Drunkard*, unknown, 100 x 140 x 280 mm

▲ 1930s, *Japanese Figure "Kojinbutsu"*, Masudaya, 75 x 105 x 220 mm

1940s, *Worker*, Germany, 105 x 60 x 95 mm

1940s, *Worker*, Germany, 90 x 90 x 50 mm

▲1930s, *Boy on Scooter*, Kuramochi, 120 x 75 x 185 mm

1940s, *Skier*, unknown, 45 x 160 x 110 mm

1940s, *Skier*, unknown, 105 x 45 x 75 mm

1930s, *Butterfly*, unknown, 143 x 95 x 35 mm

1950s, *Dragonfly*, unknown, 110 x 120 x 35 mm

1950s, *Marimba Player*, Masudaya, 90 x 85 x 145 mm

1950s, *Monkey Guitarist*, Alps, 75 x 85 x 190 mm

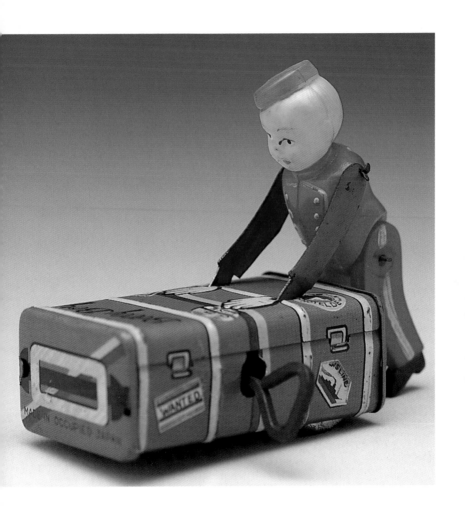

▲ 1940s, *Bell-boy*, unknown, 75 x 60 x 80 mm

1950s, *News-boy*, Nikko Kogyo, 55 x 100 x 150 mm

1950s, *Boxers*, unknown, 160 x 50 x 120 mm

1950s, *Boys Carrying Suitcases*, Alps, 70 x 55 x 110 mm

1950s, *Children Playing with Hoops*, Masudaya, 65 x 160 x 160 mm

1950s, *Sleighs*, unknown, 90 x 40 x 60, 85 x 35 x 55 mm

1940s, *Porter*, unknown, 55 x 60 x 90 mm

1940s, *Traveller*, unknown, 55 x 50 x 75 mm

1930s, *Boy with Dog*, Alps, 140 x 70 x 145 mm

1950s, *Boy with Dog*, Alps, 115 x 75 x 145 mm

◄ 1950s, *Skier*, Nikko Kogyo, 140 x 50 x 125 mm

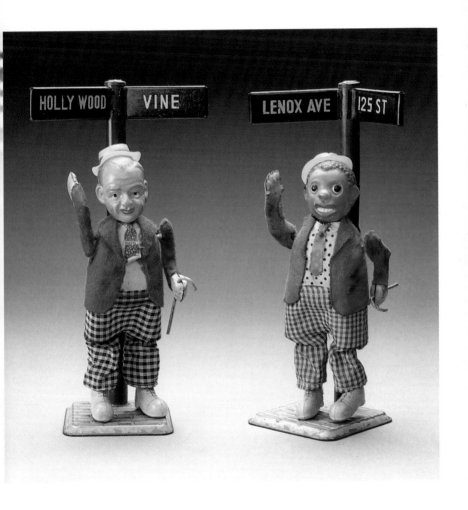

▲ 1950s, *Fred Astaire, Tap Dancer*, Alps, 75 x 110 x 210 mm

1950s, *Santa Claus in his Sleigh*, unknown, 170 x 45 x 95 mm

1950s, *Santa Claus in his Sleigh*, unknown, 190 x 60 x 90 mm

1950s, *Turkey*, unknown, 130 x 115 x 120 mm

1940s, *Peacock*, Alps, 135 x 115 x 125 mm

▲1950s, *Sparrow*, Nomura, 160 x 70 x 80 mm

950s, *Coney Island Rocket Ride*, Alps, 220 x 220 x 340 mm

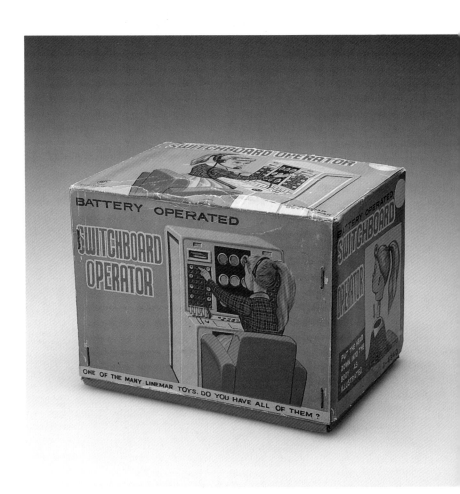

1950s, *Switchboard Operator*, Linemar, 195 x 135 x 140 mm

BATTERY OPERATED BANK
GLOBE EXPLORER

◄1950s, *Globe Explorer*, Wakasuto Boeki, 135 x 135 x 230 mm

▲1950s, *Artificial Satellite*, Swallow Toys, 100 x 213 x 160 mm

1950s, *Rabbit Drummer*, Alps, 85 x 75 x 210 mm

1950s, *Clown Juggling with his Feet*, unknown, 95 x 80 x 245 mm

1950s, *Juggling Clown*, Alps, 80 x 250 x 280 mm

1950s, *Monkey Basketballer*, Toply, 185 x 85 x 180 mm

1950s, *Hippopotamus*, Toply, 142 x 50 x 140 mm

1950s, *Penguins*, Marusan, 140 x 65 x 135 mm

1950s, *Penguin Skier*, Nomura, 110 x 70 x 120 mm

◄1950s, *Double Ferris Wheel with Swing-boats*, Asahi, 295 x 110 x 290 mm

▲1950s, *Merry-Go-Round*, Linemar, 240 x 240 x 200 mm

1950s, *Clown Violinist*, Toply, 75 x 75 x 220 mm

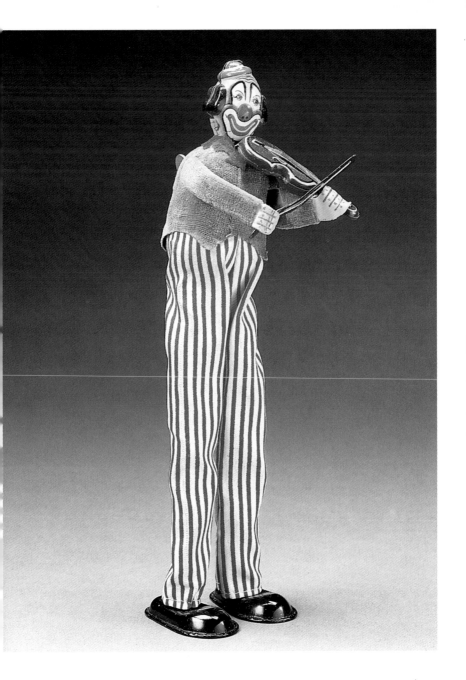

1950s, *Popeye the Roller-skater*, Line Mar, 130 x 75 x 100 mm

▲ 1950s, *Popeye and Bicycle*, *Popeye the Pilot*, Line Mar, 120 x 70 x 170, 150 x 130 x 110 mm

1950s, *Dogs*, Kanto Toy, Nomura, Kanto Toy, unknown

1950s, *Baseball Player*, Sankei 110 x 150 x 185 mm

1950s, *Cat*, Kanto Toy, 115 mm length

1950s, *Cat*, Fukuda, 135 mm length

1950s, *Cat*, unknown, 130 mm lenght

1950s, *Ministrel*, unknown

1950s, *Toyland See-Saw*, Hisimo Sangyo, 72 x 180 x 150 mm

▲ 1930s, *Elephant Balancing-act*, unknown, 80 x 180 x 120 mm

1950s, *Bulldog*, Marusan, 190 x 65 x 155 mm

1950s, *Circus Elephant*, Nomura, 120 x 90 x 280 mm

▲ 1950s, *Animal Barber*, Toply, 120 x 70 x 120 mm

1950s, *Farmer Milking his Cow*, Nikko Kogyo, 250 x 120 x 175 mm

1950s, *Ducks*, Terai, Tomiyama, Nomura, 200 x 70 x 180, 150 x 75 x 110, 130 x 60 x 130 mm

1960s, *Piggy Cook*, Yonezawa, 170 x 150 x 265 mm

1950s, *Barber Bear*, Nomura, 172 x 108 x 240 mm

BATTERY OPERATED
HOOP ZING GIRL

1950s, *Hoop Zing Girl*, Plaything, 130 x 130 x 300 mm

1950s, *Girl and Sewing-machine*, Marusan, 125 x 75 x 135 mm

1950s, *Stage-coach*, Nomura, 380 x 90 x 110 mm

1950s, *Waggon and Cowboy*, unknown, 270 x 80 x 113, 105 x 25 x 80 mm

1940s, *Circus Monkey*, unknown, 60 x 125 x 250 mm

1950s, *Monkey Pool Player*, Tohpre, 160 x 120 x 105 mm

1930s, *Fox-Hunt*, Alps, 210 x 210 x 135 mm

1950s, *Buggy Racer*, Ohta Syoten, 210 x 95 x 125 mm

▲ 1950s, *Boy and Tricycle*, unknown, 100 x 70 x 120 mm

◄ 1950s, *Jolly Clown*, Masudaya, 70 x 110 x 183 mm

▲ 1950s, *Tap Dancer*, Suzuki & Edward, 77 x 77 x 210 mm

1950s, *Marxis Toothpaste Figure*, Marxi, 60 x 55 x 105 mm

1950s, *Boy with Camera*, Nomura, 120 x 95 x 225 mm

1950s, *Cowboy Savings-box*, Yonezawa, 170 x 95 x 190 mm

1950s, *Boy and Duck*, unknown, 175 x 65 x 110 mm

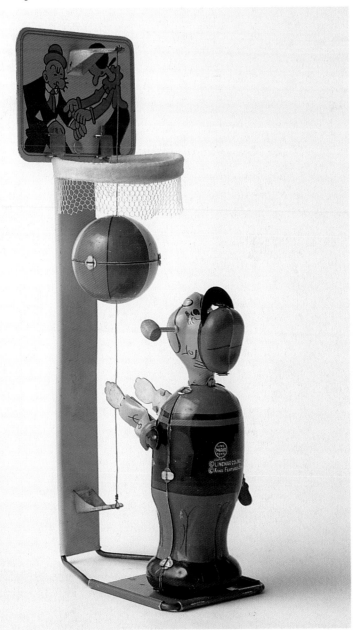

1950s, *Popeye playing Basketball*, Line Mar

▲ 1960s, *Jockey*, Haji, 205 x 70 x 175 mm

1960s, *W-3*, *Big X*, Tada, 83 x 120 x 310, 70 x 120 x 310 mm

1960s, *Batman*, Nomura, Bandai, 90 x 140 x 300, 65 x 120 x 260 mm

1960s, *Japanese Monsters*, Bull Mark, 285 x 135 x 250, 300 x 130 x 295, 285 x 130 x 280, 285 x

▲ 1960s, *Japanese Fantasy Figure "Garon"*, Nomura, 55 x 110 x 185 mm

1960s, *Japanese Fantasy Figures "Yusei Kamen"*, Nomura, 85 x 135 x 300, 63 x 105 x 205 mm

1960s, *Fantasy Figure "Maguma Taishi"*, Tada, Nomura, 82 x 140 x 330, 90 x 135 x 300 mm

1960s, *Eightman*, Yonezawa, 90 x 195 x 230 mm

1960s, *Big X*, Nomura, 135 x 85 x 310 mm

1960s, *Tetsuwan Atom*, Nomura, 85 x 175 x 305 mm

1960s, *Fantasy Figure "Par Man"*, Bandai, 80 x 130 x 270 mm

Cars & Bikes

1910s, *Classic Car*, Y. Suzuki, 175 x 100 x 120 mm

1920s, *Side-car*, unknown, 180 x 120 x 110 mm

1910s, *Motor Tricycle*, H. Yamada, 190 x 70 x 125 mm

1920s, *Classic Auto*, unknown, 150 x 70 x 82 mm

1920s, *Automobile Sedan*, unknown, 175 x 70 x 80 mm

1920s, *Automobile Sedan*, unknown, 250 x 190 x 110 mm

920s, *Tank*, unknown, 105 x 48 x 55 mm

1900s, *Automobile*, unknown, 160 x 80 x 90 mm

1920s, *Automobile Sedan*, Masudaya, 250 x 190 x 110 mm

1920s, *Racing Car*, unknown, 135 x 70 x 65 mm

1930s, *Open Car*, unknown, 300 x 100 x 200 mm

1930s, *Gasoline Truck*, Nomura, 230 x 100 x 120 mm

1920s, *Open Car*, Toyodo, 165 x 80x 75 mm

1930s, *Racing Car*, unknown, 190 x 80 x 85 mm

1930s, *Fire-engine*, Tomiyama, 250 x 90 x 180 mm

1950s, *Fire-engine*, Masudaya, Line Mar, 140 x 80 x 100, 108 x 70 x 75 mm

1930s, *Children's Bus*, Tomiyama, 235 x 115 x 90 mm

1920s, *Open Car*, unknown, 180 x 80 x 100 mm

1930s, *Topsy-Turvy Tom*, Masudaya, 220 x 135 x 115 mm

1950s, *Police Bikes with Side-cars*, Yonezawa, 120 x 75 x 80, 120 x 110 x 85 mm

930s, *Army Motor Bikes*, T.Y.D.Y., unknown, 160 x 55 x 95, 120 x 35 x 75 mm

1930s, *Tank*, unknown, 95 x 40 x 50 mm

1930s, *Tank*, unknown, 280 x 110 x 135 mm

1930s, *Automobile*, Masudaya, 325 x 100 x 80 mm

1930s, *Side-car*, Masudaya, 230 x 190 x 100 mm

950s, *Motor Bike*, unknown

1930s, *Classic Car*, Tomiyama, 190 x 80 x 70 mm

1930s, *Auto "Star" Model*, Kohno Kakuzo, 210 x 110 x 100 mm

1930s, *Automobile Sedan*, unknown, 270 x 195 x 105 mm

1930s, *Classic Car*, unknown, 260 x 110 x 105 mm

1930s, *Tank*, Tomiyama, 350 x 145 x 155 mm

1930s, *Tank*, unknown, 255 x 110 x 130 mm

1940s, *Jeep*, Kosuge Toys, 105 x 45 x 68 mm

1940s, *Motor Cycle*, Masudaya, 125 x 55 x 95 mm

1940s, *Car*, unknown, 100 x 50 x 40 mm

1940s, *Mercury*, unknown, 150 x 60 x 50 mm

1940s, *Cars*, unknown, 170 x 70 x 55, 100 x 50 x 40 mm

1940s, *Car*, unknown, 155 x 65 x 50 mm

1940s, *Car*, unknown, 170 x 70 x 55 mm

1940s, *Car*, Taico, 160 x 60 x 45 mm

1940s, *Car*, Taico, 160 x 60 x 45 mm

1940s, *Scooter*, Kuramochi, 100 x 50 x 105 mm

1950s, *"Rabbit" Scooter*, unknown, 145 x 50 x 110 mm

1950s, *Gas Station and Car*, Yonezawa, 130 x 240 x 95 mm

1950s, *Remote-controlled Car*, Line Mar, 245 x 110 x 100 mm

1950s, *Remote-controlled Car*, Line Mar, 185 x 75 x 75 mm

1950s, *Packard*, Alps, 400 x 160 x 120 mm

950s, *1954 Pontiac Star Chief*, Asahi, 250 x 105 x 80 mm

1950s, *1954 Pontiac Star Chief*, Ashai, 250 x 105 x 80 mm

1950s, *1956 Mercury Custom*, Alps, 240 x 100 x 75 mm

1950s, *Buick*, unknown, 230 x 95 x 75 mm

1950s, *1956 Oldsmobile Super 88*, Masudaya, 350 x 150 x 105 mm

1950s, *Mercedes-Benz Racer*, Marusan, 260 x 100 x 75 mm

1950s, *Mercedes-Benz Racer*, Marusan, 260 x 100 x 75 mm

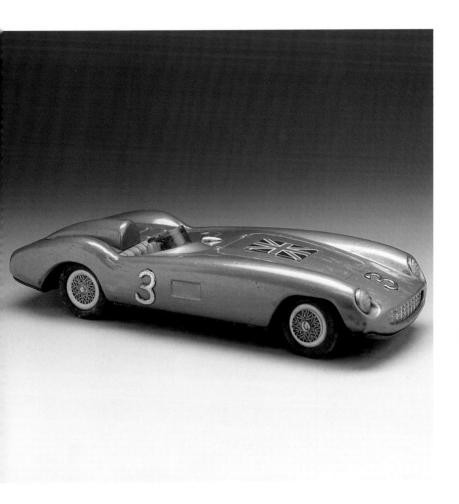

1950s, *Ferrari*, Bandai, 209 x 83 x 45 mm

1950s, *Volkswagen Construction Kit*, Masudaya

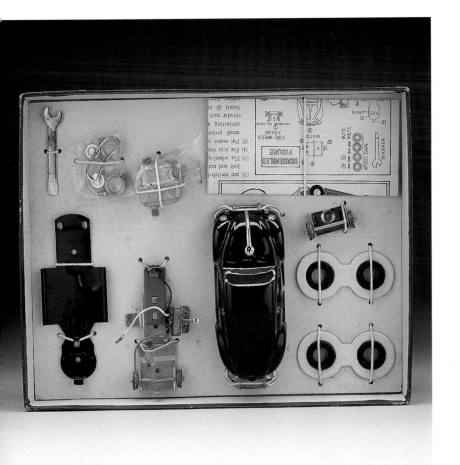

1950s, *Atom Car*, Yonezawa, 410 x 170 x 130 mm

1950s, *Scooters*, Marusan, 150 x 65 x 110 mm

950s, *Motor Tricycle*, Sankei, 145 x 50 x 65 mm

1950s, *Tractor*, Nomura, 260 x 120 x 160 mm

950s, *Robot Bulldozer*, Line Mar, 235 x 145 x 165 mm

1950s, *MG*, Marusan, 315 x 65 x 100 mm

1950s, *1954 Lincoln*, Yonezawa, 325 x 125 x 100 mm

1950s, *Lincoln*, Masudaya, 340 x 175 x 105 mm

1950s, *Oldsmobile*, unknown, 350 x 150 x 105 mm

950s, *1958 Edsel Citation*, Asahi, 278 x 114 x 80 mm

1950s, *Fire-engine*, Yonezawa, 135 x 50 x 70 mm

1950s, *Fire-engine*, Kokyu Shokai, 180 x 60 x 65 mm

1950s, *"Wonderful" Bus,* Yonezawa, 440 x 120 x 120 mm

1950s, *Omnibus*, Kaname, 305 x 90 x 100 mm

1950s, *Circus Truck*, Yoshi, 250 x 60 x 95 mm

1950s, *1958 Buick Century*, Yonezawa, 295 x 125 x 85 mm

1950s, *1956 Chrysler New Yorker*, Alps, 350 x 140 x 95 mm

1950s, *Scooter*, Koshibe, 200 x 55 x 130 mm

1950s, *"King" Scooter*, Yonezawa, 225 x 55 x 155 mm

1950s, *Mitsubishi Three-wheel Pick-up*, Bandai, 300 x 95 x 100 mm

1950s, *Orient Three-wheel Pick-up*, Yonezawa, 225 x 85 x 90 mm

1950s, *Baggage Truck*, Masudaya, 190 x 95 x 170 mm

1950s, *Futuristic Car*, Yonezawa, 270 x 100 x 70 mm

1950s, *1953 Chevrolet Corvette*, Bandai, 180 x 75 x 60 mm

950s, *GM Turbine Car*, Asahi, 225 x 85 x 70 mm

1950s, *Cadillac*, Marusan, 310 x 125 x 95 mm

1950s, *Cadillac*, Marusan, 315 x 125 x 95 mm

1950s, *Atom Jet*, Yonezawa, 200 x 66 x 185 mm

1950s, *Volvo P.V. 444*, K.S. Toy, 190 x 75 x 65 mm

1950s, *1958 Edsel Corsair*, unknown, 270 x 105 x 80 mm

950s, *Lincoln Mark III Continental*, Bandai, 295 x 100 x 75 mm

1960s, *1959 Renault 4 CV Hino*, Yonezawa, 195 x 75 x 70 mm

1950s, *Volvo P.V. 444*, K.S. Toy, 190 x 75 x 65 mm

1960s, *Porsche 356 B*, Kaname Sangyo, 195 x 80 x 73 mm

950s, *Car*, unknown, 280 x 115 x 85 mm

1960s, *Rolls-Royce Silver Cloud*, unknown, 260 x 95 x 95 mm

1950s, *Cadillac Convertible*, Alps, 290 x 110 x 75 mm

1950s, *Meguro Motor Bike*, Bandai, 300 x 130 x 147 mm

1950s, *"J.T.Y. Lucky Bus"*, Yonezawa, 230 x 75 x 80 mm

950s, *"Sunny Bus"*, Nihon Boeki, 245 x 55 x 75 mm

1950s, *Fire-engine*, Yoshiya, 425 x 120 x 180 mm

1950s, *1954 Chevrolet Bel-Air*, Marusan, 280 x 125 x 95 mm

950s, *Cadillac*, Marusan, 310 x 125 x 95 mm

1950s, *Motor Bikes*, Koshibe, Nikko Gangu Kogyo, Yoshiya, Yonezawa
125 x 55 x 85, 115 x 50 x 75, 115 x 55 x 75, 115 x 50 x 90 mm

1950s, *Jaguar XK 150*, Bandai, 245 x 100 x 70 mm

1950s, *1956 Ford Thunderbird*, unknown, 285 x 110 x 80 mm

1950s, *Million Bus*, Kaname, 305 x 90 x 100 mm

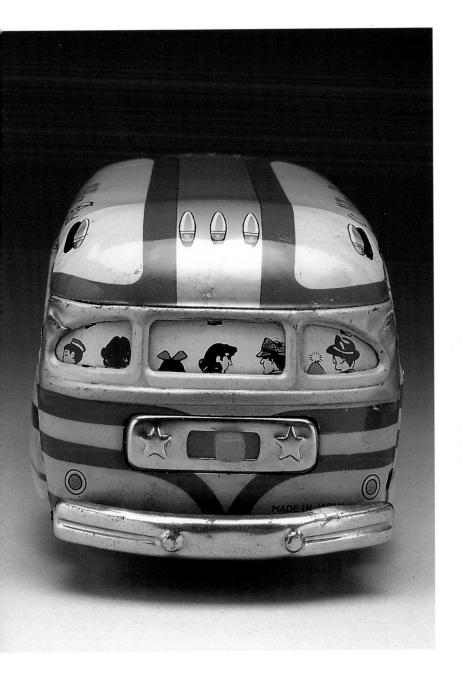

1950s, *Omnibus*, Nomura, 210 x 66 x 70 mm

1950s, *Fire-engine*, Marusan, 400 x 120 x 180 mm

1950s, *Steamroller*, Yonezawa, 175 x 90 x 105 mm

◄ 1950s, *Man in Classic Auto*, Masudaya, 180 x 100 x 150 mm

▲ 1950s, *Men in Classic Auto*, Yonezawa, 230 x 120 x 180, 180 x 100 x 150 mm

1950s, *Space Bus*, Usagiya, 350 x 95 x 120 mm

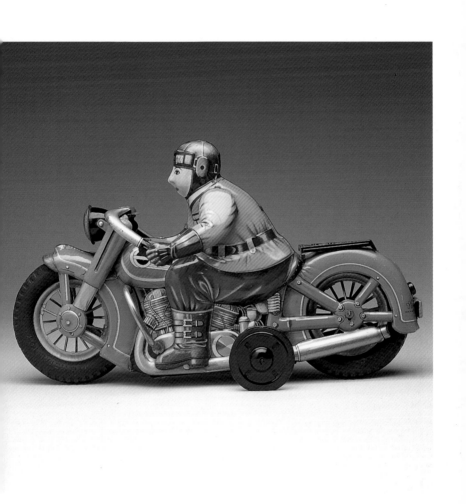

950s, *Harley Davidson Motor Bike*, I.Y. Metal Toys, 360 x 120 x 220 mm

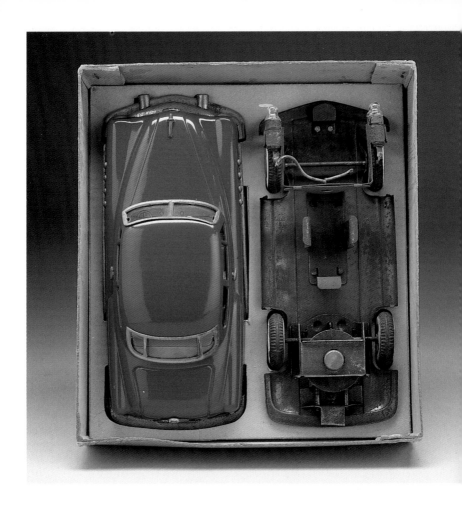

1950s, *1953 Buick Roadmaster Construction Kit*, Marusan, 85 x 80 x 60 mm

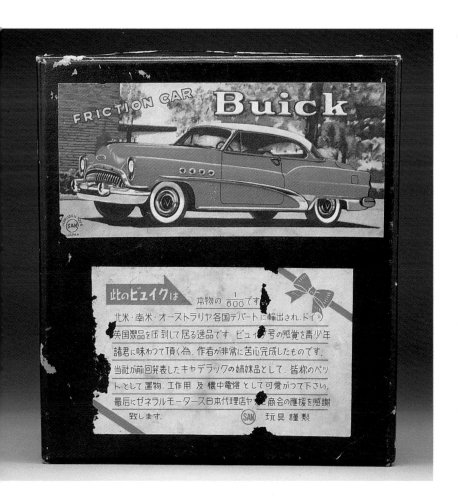

1950s, *Volkswagen with Oval Windows*, Masudaya, 195 x 80 x 125 mm

950s, *Citroen 2 CV*, Daiya, 210 x 75 x 80 mm

1950s, *U.S. Army Jeep*, Nihon Boeki, 260 x 115 x 115, 260 x 110 x 115 mm

950s, *Jeep*, unknown, 210 x 95 x 110 mm

1950s, *TV Crew Bus and Car*, Tomiyama, unknown, 215 x 90 x 155, 190 x 75 x 115 mm

1950s, *Fire-engine*, unknown, 175 x 55 x 80 mm

1950s, *1957 Ford Pick-Up*, Bandai, 305 x 110 x 95 mm

950s, *Ford Pick-Up*, Bandai, 305 x 110 x 95 mm

1950s, *Dream Car*, Ichiko, 200 x 80 x 75 mm

1950s, *Pontiac Dream Car*, Mitsuhashi, 255 x 95 x 65 mm

1950s, *Three-wheel Pick-ups*, Bandai, Bandai, Yonezawa,
210 x 95 x 90, 260 x 95 x 100, 225 x 85 x 90 mm

1950s, *Daihatsu Midget*, Kokyu Shokai, 165 x 70 x 95 mm

1950s, *Mazda Pick-up K360*, Bandai, 190 x 85 x 88 mm

1950s, *Dream Car*, Line Mar, 290 x 130 x 70 mm

1950s, *Lincoln Futura*, Alps, 280 x 125 x 85 mm

1950s, *Mercedes-Benz 300*, Alps, 240 x 95 x 75 mm

1950s, *Motor Bike*, I.Y. Metal Toys, 300 x 100 x 175 mm

1950s, *Volvo Amazon*, K.S. Toy, 230 x 90 x 80 mm

1950s, *Space Patrol Car and Box*, Ichiko, 217 x 85 x 82 mm

1950s, *1952 Cadillac 62*, Alps, 290 x 110 x 75 mm

1950s, *1954 Cadillac*, Nomura, 340 x 150 x 105 mm

950s, *1956 Ford Fairlane*, Bandai, 305 x 114 x 85 mm

1950s, *Toyota Crown*, Bandai, Asahi, 207 x 75 x 69, 206 x 80 x 70 mm

950s, *Toyota Crown*, Bandai, 207 x 75 x 69 mm

1950s, *Messerschmitt KR 200*, Bandai, 200 x 95 x 90 mm

1950s, *1959 Cadillac*, Bandai, 280 x 105 x 75 mm

1950s, *1958 Lincoln Mark III Continental*, Bandai, 295 x 105 x 75 mm

1950s, *Fire-engine*, Koshibe, 195 x 105 x 105 mm

1950s, *Fire-engine*, Marusan, 175 x 70 x 90 mm

1950s, *Fire-engine*, Momoya, 190 x 80 x 85 mm

1950s, *1959 Cadillac Eldorado*, Bandai, 280 x 105 x 75 mm

1950s, *Volvo*, K.S. Toy, 230 x 90 x 80 mm

1950s, *Buick*, unknown, 260 x 120 x 90 mm

1950s, *Convertibles*, Nihon Boeki, 200 x 85 x 70 mm

1960s, 1950s, *Mazda R 360*, *Renault*, Bandai, Yonezawa, 180 x 80 x 75, 195 x 75 x 70 mm

1950s, *Austin Cambridge A50 (Nissan)*, Kokyu-Shokai, 200 x 80 x 76 mm

1950s, *Mercedes-Benz 300 SL*, Marusan, 225 x 97 x 65 mm

1950s, *Mercedes-Benz 300 SL*, Tsukuda, 232 x 93 x 72 mm

1950s, *Buick Le Sabre*, Yonezawa, 200 x 75 x 55 mm

1950s, *Omnibus*, Nihon Boeki, 218 x 60 x 62 mm

1950s, *Omnibus*, Naito Shoten, 298 x 92 x 82 mm

1950s, *Motor Cycle with Side-car*, Marusan, 120 x 220 x 120 mm

1950s, *Omnibus*, Marusan, 370 x 90 x 120 mm

1950s, *Ambulance*, Masudaya, 190 x 80 x 58 mm

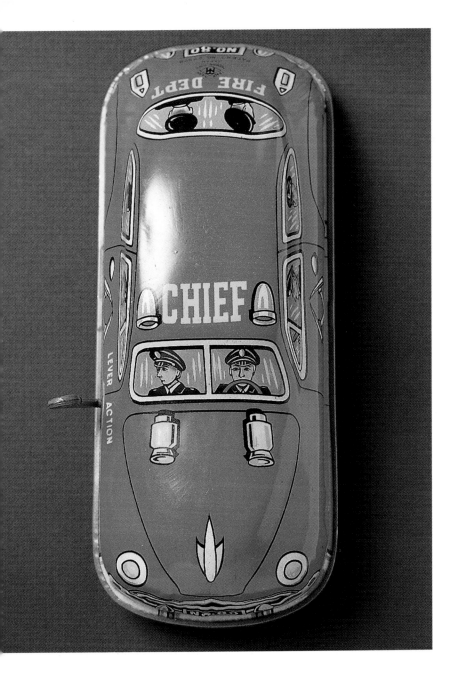

950s, *Fire Dept. Car*, Masudaya, 163 x 78 x 53 mm

1950s, *Mitsubishi Three Wheel Pick-up*, Bandai, 260 x 95 x 100 mm

1950s, *Mazda Three-wheel Pick-up,* Bandai, 210 x 95 x 90 mm

1930s, *Gasoline Truck*, Masudaya, 220 x 80 x 100 mm

1950s, *Packard*, Alps, 170 x 400 x 120 mm

1950s, *1956 Mercury Custom*, Alps, 240 x 100 x 75 mm

1950s, *1953 Cadillac*, Nomura, 340 x 150 x 105 mm

950s, *Military Police Motor Bike*, Masudaya, 170 x 50 x 120 mm

1950s, *Mazda Three-wheel Pick-up*, Bandai, 210 x 95 x 90 mm

950s, *Daihatsu Three-wheel Pick-up*, Nomura, 270 x 90 x 90 mm

1950s, *Racing Car*, Tomiyama, 250 x 120 x 115 mm

1950s, *Car*, Alps, 400 x 170 x 120 mm

1950s, *Toyota Crown Deluxe*, Bandai, 230 x 90 x 78 mm

950s, *1954 MG TF*, Bandai, 210 x 85 x 80 mm

950s, *Cars with Pop-up Parts*, Nihon Boeki, 200 x 85 x 70 mm

1950s, *1957 Lincoln Mark II Continental*, Line Mar, 290 x 105 x 80

Farm Tractor Set

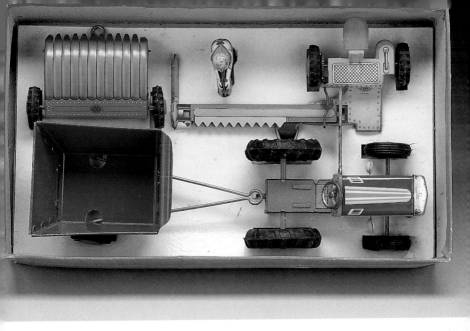

1950s, *Farm Tractor Set*, Masudaya

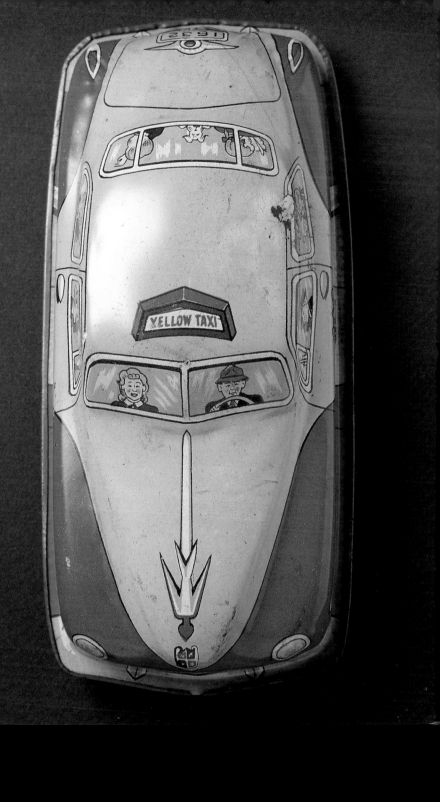

1950s, *Car*, Alps, 400 x 170 x 120 mm

1950s, *1956 Toyopet Crown RS*, Asahi, 206 x 80 x 70 mm

1950s, *Pegasus Deluxe*, Yonezawa, 220 x 100 x 70 mm

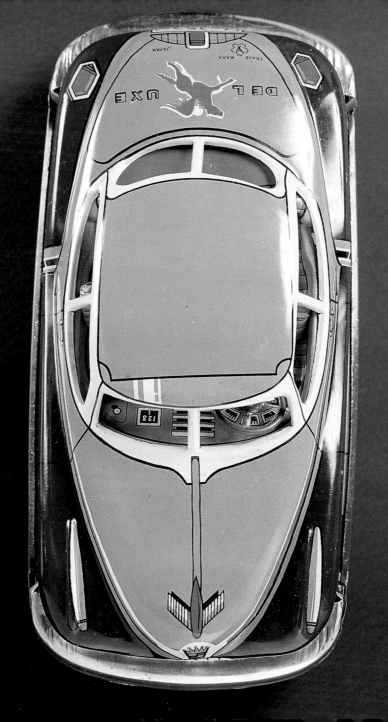

1950s, *Van*, Marusan, 240 x 95 x 125 mm

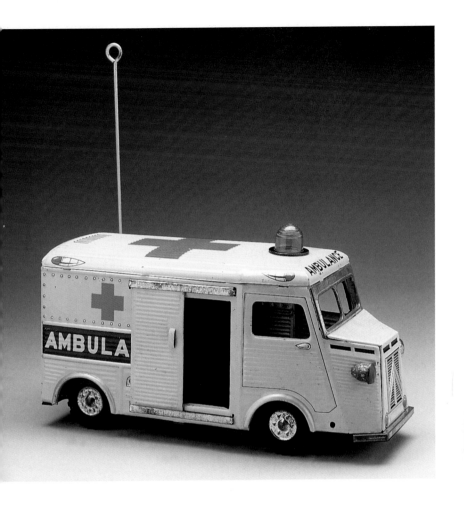

1950s, *Citroen Ambulance*, unknown, 190 x 120 x 110 mm

1950s, *Aston Martin*, unknown, 280 x 120 x 140 mm

1950s, *MG*, Bandai, 210 x 85 x 80 mm

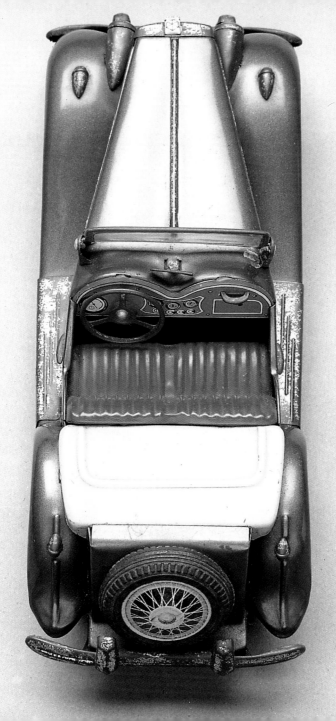

1950s, *1958 Triumph TR 3A*, Bandai, 215 x 80 x 70 mm

950s, *Cadillac*, unknown, 170 x 70 x 55 mm

1965, *Volkswagen Karmann-Ghia*, Bandai, 190 x 78 x 57 mm

1960s, *Renault Caravelle*, Asahi, 230 x 95 x 75 mm

◄ 1960s, *Mercedes-Benz 220S*, Bandai, 265 x 100 x 80 mm

▲ 1960s, *Citroen DS 19*, Bandai, 300 x 110 x 90 mm

1960s, *Batmobile*, Masudaya, 310 x 100 x 105 mm

1960s, *Batmobile*, Yanoman, 152 x 95 x 103 mm

1960s, *Batmobile*, Aoshin, 300 x 105 x 90 mm

1960s, *Family House Trailer*, Bandai, 315 x 95 x 180 mm

◄1960s, *Cadillac Eldorado*, Bandai, 290 x 100 x 75 mm

▲ 1960s, *Buick*, Ichiko, 455 x 165 x 110 mm

1960s, *Cadillac*, Yonezawa, 550 x 195 x 123 mm

1960s, *Imperial*, Asahi, 150 x 390 x 100 mm

1960s, *E-Type Jaguar*, Tomiyama, 310 x 115 x 80 mm

1960s, *Ferrari*, Bandai, 286 x 100 x 78 mm

1960s, *BMW Isetta (Four-wheel)*, Bandai, 70 x 100 x 95 mm

Teruhisa Kitahara

Born 1948 in Tokyo, Japan
Graduated from the Department of
Economics of Aoyama University
Tin toy collector of world-wide renown
Owner of Toys, Inc.
Curator of Tin Toys Museum

Geboren 1948 in Tokio, Japan
Wirtschaftswissenschaftliches
Studium an der Aoyama Universität
Blechspielzeugsammler von inter-
nationalem Ruf
Besitzer von Toys, Inc.
Kurator des Tin Toys Museum

Né en 1948 à Tokyo, Japon
Diplômé en sciences économiques
de l'Aoyama University
Collectionneur de jouets en fer-blanc
de renommée mondiale
Propriétaire de Tin Toys Inc.
Conservateur du Tin Toys Museum

Yukio Shimizu

Born 1944 in Tokyo, Japan
Graduated from Photography Department, Art Center College of Design
Active in various areas of art, including
commercial films and magazines
Strives to capture the essence of his
subjects by means of accurate,
intelligent images

Geboren 1944 in Tokio, Japan
Fotografiestudium am Art Center
College of Design
Auf verschiedenen künstlerischen
Gebieten tätig, u. a. Arbeiten für
Werbefilme und Magazine
Versucht auf intelligente Weise, in
präzisen Bildern die wahre Natur
seiner Themen einzufangen

Né en 1944 à Tokyo, Japon
Diplôme de photographie à l'Art
Center College of Design
Travaille dans différents domaines
artistiques, y compris le cinéma
publicitaire et la presse magazines
S'efforce toujours de saisir la véritable
nature de ses sujets par ses photographies précises et intelligentes